MW00464206

Recognizing God

Shaman Wisdom Teacher

Winged Wolf HHC

Higher Consciousness Books

1998

Cover Portrait by Judy Galvan taken in the Happy House.

Winged Wolf, The Jeweled Path of Living Wisdom, The Academy of Shamanic Study and Exploration, Shamanic Traveler, Shamanic Empowerment Program, Soul Vision, Companion Energy, Ancient Art of Looking, The Shamanic Path of Living as Soul, The Shamanic Path of Living Wisdom, The Path of Soul, Soul Circle, and Wisdom Eye Circle are registered trademarks/tradename, among others.

Higher Consciousness Books
Division of Coastline Publishing Company
Post Office Box 250
Deer Harbor, Washington 98243 USA
Phone/Fax (360) 376-3700
E-Mail: tspolw@rockisland.com

Printed in the United States of America

Library of Congress Catalog No.: 98-085948
ISBN: 0-932927-13-0

Dedication

To the lineage of Primordial Spiritual Masters....
and to all those apprentices who contributed
their efforts to the production of this book,
for they are the continuum of this
great lineage, in training.

Preface

In a moment you will enter a pathway, a passage that will lead you to the Wish-fulfilling Kingdom.... a land (consciousness) where you will *see* the blending of the ONEness of all things. The Path you are about to travel is jeweled, because as you read.... a few words, then a few more words, all of a sudden many words may begin to resonate in you, triggering snatches of long ago memories.... memories from a time when the treasured mind teachings were a part of your life. The words then, magically become jewels of wisdom - an affirmation you are on the right track.

You may experience *Recognizing God* as a book like no other found, because as each sentence, paragraph and chapter begins to resonate and expand in you.... expanding weeks and even months after putting the book down, an awakening <u>as Soul</u> will emerge. And as Winged Wolf's words, (the Primordial Teachings) continue to deepen in you, in an instant, you may just wake-up and *Live* in the most powerful and glorious place.... The Present Moment.

Recognizing God does not introduce a new doctrine or creed; but rather, presents a new 'impulse' and clarity to the Primordial Teachings.... recognizing and *realizing* the Godhead in each of us. **God Realization is attainable.** It begins by first Recognizing God.

I pray that Winged Wolf's work may reach and benefit as many hüm-an beings as possible.

Loving Crow
Apprentice to Winged Wolf

"When you become one with the teachings, then you know they are no longer something from a book; they are a part of your life, a part of you."

From chapter, *Arenas of Clarity*

Contents

Sitting in Silence

by
Presenter of Joy
Gretchen DeGeer
Apprentice to Winged Wolf

Holding soft vision
through peripheral view,
quits the mind
letting energy through.

Look and listen,
only to observe,
without judging
others worth

Feel the energy
in all you see,
letting life
freely be.

Looking "in" to mentalize
prevents an outward flow
that invites joyful surprise,
making life gold.

Introduction

The Jeweled Path of Living Wisdom is a Path that leads the aspirant along the footsteps required to attain the realization of the God-Self. It begins with access to the Primordial Mind-Treasure Teachings or access to the indestructible gems of Primordial Wisdom, which propel one's life toward clarity and freedom. These basis footsteps are introduced as:

◇ The Written Teachings, and contemplation of the written teachings;

◇ Linkage with a Realized Master of the Teachings;

◇ Self-Discipline;

◇ The Oral Teachings and Initiation received from the Realized Master whom you have linked to;

◇ Impeccability to the Teachings and your Realized Master;

◇ Recognition of Soul and/or the God-Self;

◇ God Realization.

Recognizing God is a transliteral transmission of the primordial teachings from the primordial lineage of spiritual masters, however, it is not copied or paraphrased from ancient texts (yet exists in ancient texts); but, instead, is recorded from the well-spring of silent knowledge whispered from the ancient source ItSelf, The Void or God. The Mind-Treasure Teachings begin to unfold in this way in an individual when impeccability takes root in the aspirant and he or she makes choices that lead beyond dualities. At this point a commitment is made to live as an expression of The Teachings and to share the

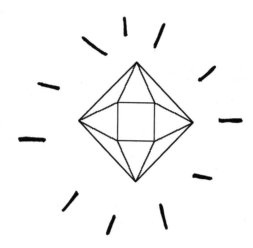

expression with as many others that are willing to listen. This commitment is simultaneous to God-Realization.

It is not important for a spiritual master's life to simulate the lives of other spiritual masters, only to follow the heart-beat of The Teachings as they are enlivened in his or her personal being. It is through this personalized enlivenment that others are attracted to the Path and Its jeweled teachings. This means that The Teacher may be a singular person or a householder, devoid of attachment, including lust, anger, greed and vanity. It is a commitment made and acted upon, free from an intention of personal gain and free from consummation of fear. Once the commitment is effected, The Teacher is then ripe to receive the Mind-Treasure Teachings and to pass Them on to those who are seeking enlightenment. Thus, we arrive at the purpose of this book. Most of its text was spoken to advanced apprentices, from questions that arose through a daily observance of The Teachings by those who visited me at the property Between the Wind. The apprentices who appear in the text were those who were visiting at the time, and to preserve their privacy, only their power name is used.

Each text contains a key phrase(s) that unlocks an aspect of the mysterious parallax needed to *Recognize God*. These phrases act like time bombs that tick away inside the reader until he or she links up with a live spiritual master who will stimulate a life situation that will burst forth into the individual's realization of the nature and identity of God or The Void. The adventure begins.

With Great Love as Soul....

Winged Wolf

Remember Me

Winged Wolf: "I want to talk about *receiving* the teachings.

"It is easy to listen to the teachings and say, *'Oh yes, Oh yes, I know that. This is right. Oh, Isn't that wonderful. I am so happy to hear it. Oh, how liberating, how wonderful, wonderful,'* and walk away feeling that the teachings have been given to you, and feeling, *oh,* so empowered. But, the real way to receive the teachings, comes from taking them into your life, and from living them.

"For instance, once upon a time, there was an apprentice who was asked to take care of her body, which was in very bad condition. She was told specific things to do for specific problems. Of course, once done, the problems then cleared up. *'Oh well, I don't have those problems anymore, so I guess what was told me no longer matters. You know, I am superperson now.'* She put aside what she had learned, and her ailments came back.

"This is the way healings work. Until a person has integrated the spiritual knowledge into their lives and makes it a part of their lives, she cannot get well. That goes for bad knees, (Winged Wolf looks at Loving Crow, who is sitting in the back of the Happy House with an ice pack on her knee), or any other kind of problem that a person would have.... lack of abundance, or being sick all the time. Any problem that hangs onto a person cannot be cured or healed, until the remedy is *integrated* into one's life. It is the integration of a remedy.... taking home what has been learned and applying it to one's life, that becomes a healing salve to a wound.

"Now, sometimes the teachings are given to someone and they begin to shake inside, from their resistance to the teachings, because he knows that the teaching is going to have a transforming experience, if he accepts it....... And it is true, that teaching, because it resonates so strongly in him, sets up that resistance in him, and as he accepts it, it is going to shake the very foundation of his life and transform him.

"You know, I used to be terrified of the teachings as an apprentice myself. I can remember saying to Alana, my Sioux Shaman teacher, how I was terrified that she and the teachings were going to possess me. She, of course, looked at me in astonishment, *'Would **that** be so bad?'* she asked.

"There is nothing else to life. When you come to a certain place in your spiritual unfoldment, there *is* nothing else. You can turn your back on the teachings; you can hide, and do other things; you can go back to old habit patterns, but the teachings are sitting on your shoulder, giving you little taps,

> *'Remember me.....*
> *Remember me.....*
> *Remember me.....*

There is absolute stillness in the Happy House as Winged Wolf slowly repeats,

> *'Remember me....*

"You can keep ignoring the teachings, but you are aware of them at the same time. You can persist in doing things in the old way, but the teachings keep tapping you on the shoulder saying,

> *'Remember me.....*
> *Remember me.....*

Remember me.....

"Then one day, you may die of sickness or old age, or whatever, and on the astral planes the teachings are calling,

> *'Remember me......*
> *Remember me......*

and you ignore them all the same.

"Until one day, a situation lines up on the physical plane and you are sucked back into life.... and you open your eyes and the teachings are calling,

> *'Remember me.....*
> *Remember me.....*

And all your life, you feel lonely. It is that little missing piece, *'Oh, I am so different than everybody else.'* That feeling of difference is the teachings sitting on your shoulder calling,

> *'Remember me....*
> *Remember me....*

"You can have such a longing to remember, but all you have is this little nudge that calls,

> *'Remember me....*
> *Remember me....*

And you can't even remember what it is you are trying to remember. There is a terrible longing, a terrible longing... to everything that comes up, and you try to listen, and you say to yourself, *'Oh,*

> *Remember me....*
> > *Remember me.....*

Oh, no! No! I don't want to remember you, it hurts me.' So, you begin to distance yourself more and more from the *'remember me'* tap. You try to say, *'No, no, I am not going to listen to the.....*

'Remember me....
> *Remember me...*

It is the loneliness that makes me feel too alone..... too different..... too separated. I can't ...... because I have this physical problem. You know, if I eat something, it will make me sick. If I take in this memory, this little bit of teaching, and remember it, it will make me sick. What will happen to me? Maybe, I will lose everything..... maybe all my material fortune; or maybe my husband won't love me anymore, or my wife will run away...... **'No, no, I won't.....** *Remember me... I won't, Remember me.'* Winged Wolf responds very quietly by softly whispering to such inner thoughts saying,

> *'Remember me......*
> > *Remember me.....*
> > > *Remember me.....*

There is no such remember me.... There is no such remember me. There is no such remember me.' Again Winged Wolf repeats,

> *'Remember me....*

Remember me....
Remember me.

"The longing gets so great that the person develops allergies to life. Life itself has become so unbearable in so many ways, and all through this unbearableness of life, there is still,

'*Remember me......*
Remember me....

"It is a haunting feeling now. It is so subtle, sitting on your shoulder, haunting, haunting,

'*Remember me.....*
Remember me.....
Remember me.....

Winged Wolf continues with a whisper,

'*Remember me...............*
Remember me............
Remember me..........

"Then the person continues on with their life, and the environment and situations begin to have such an impact, that everything makes him sick, and uncomfortable. And inside, there is a part that fights back and says, '*I won't put up with this. I won't tolerate this,*' and he rejects more of life, he rejects more food, more associations, more everything.... Everything is rejected. A sense of compassion is gone. He is pushing all of life away from him. He is pushing away love, but clinging to security.... *pushing away love but clinging to security....* pushing away love but clinging to security and, all along, there is this haunting feeling.... haunting feeling that says,

> *'Remember me.....*
> *Remember me.....*

'Oh this horrible nagging aching lonely feeling.....'

Quietly Winged Wolf whispers,

> *'Remember me.....*
> *Remember me......*

"Then the person comes to old age and sickness, and dies.....

> *'Remember me.....*
> *Remember me.....*

"In the astral plane, the loneliest place, where time seems like eternity, ...

> *'Remember me.....*

Winged Wolf faintly repeats,

> *'Remember me....*
> *Remember......*

"Then a situation occurs and the person is drawn back into life to deal with problems left from his past incarnation. He is back again, beginning life by pushing it away..... beginning life by pushing it away.... beginning life by pushing it away. *'No, I don't want to be hurt. No, I can't be a part of this. No, I am different than everybody else. I am so different. Nobody understands me. I am different. I am so different than everybody else.'* And the loneliness sets in, and the sound of the loneliness is....

> *'Remember me...*
> *Remember me....*

"Occasionally, the person meets a teacher who looks at them and knows their pain, but because he is resisting the teacher and asking for help at the same time, the teacher can only offer love and compassion, to listen, to hear the song, that haunts him,

> *'Remember me.....*
> *Remember me......*

"And the person continues on their way to finish that lifetime and, when he comes back again, because he met someone who did offer divine love, even though he rejected it, the memory lingers, an energy about *The Teacher's* face or a look in their eye, and that reminds him....

> *'Remember me.........*

"And then, the person enters a new life looking for love, still pushing people away but moving in-between those they push away, hearing the song of

> *'Remember me......*

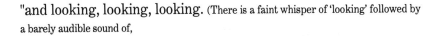

"and looking, looking, looking. (There is a faint whisper of 'looking' followed by a barely audible sound of,

> *'Remember me.....*
>   *Remember me......'*

In the silence between Winged Wolf's *'Remember me'*, apprentices experience an energy vibration that becomes a gateway for them to experience the enlivening of Soul and the **Oneness As Soul** in the repeated words,

> *'Remember me.....*
>   *Remember me.....*
>   *Remember me.....*

The Happy House is filled with an awareness of divine love.

"And one day the person finds *The Teacher's* gaze in someone else's eyes, and the individual feels the compassion and love that is *living* in those eyes, to hear the song,

> *'Remember me.....*
>   *Remember me.....*
>   *Remember me.....*

..... and it frightens the one so much, he runs away feeling ever more lonely.

> *'Remember me......*
>   *Remember me..........*

"The song becomes so loud and haunting,

'*Remember me.......*
             Remember me.......
                    Remember me.......

"And again death comes, **and** again the melody of

      '*Remember me.......*
             Remember me.......
                    Remember me.......

"And then he is reborn, hearing the song a little louder than the previous time, because he never forgot the *look* of love and compassion.... even though he ran from it............. He listens and mingles among the crowds, aggressively seeking the eyes of the one who said,

      '*Re----member------me.....*
        Re-----member------me.'

"And he begins to realize that the eyes of the one that said '*Remember me'* were the teachings alive in that embodiment. And again, he finds *The Teacher* who looks back at him with divine love and compassion, and this time, he does not run. He stands in front of *The Teacher*, and he shakes and shivers, and the song of '*Remember me'* is so loud all around. He shakes, shivers, and shakes and shivers, never moving towards but not moving back, and he shakes and shivers hearing,
      '*Remember me.....*
        Remember me...

"The song gets stronger and he begins to hear bits and pieces of the teachings. He shakes and shivers, he shakes and shivers --

'Remember me....
Remember me.....

"And one day he stops shaking, and he stops shivering. He may have to die again first to get to that point, but one day he stops running all together and he stops shaking and shivering, which is just another form of running. He sits to listen to the song of,

'Remember me....
Remember me...

"as it is coming through in the embodiment of the teaching, and he accepts; but you see, it takes all of that to prepare. You have been through all of those stages to be here; so, never be hard on yourselves. You are giants among men, hüm-an.

"You are the evolvement of yourself, awakening to the song of

'Remember me....
Remember me.

(A Very long pause............................)

"May the blessings be."

Kookaburra: "How do we recognize the 'Remember me'?"

"The teachings are locked inside of you. They are a part of you, as Soul, and when you look at someone who is living as Soul, you remember. That is what *remember* means.

"Everyone is Soul. We are all the same as Soul. Some remember more than others. The only difference between one who remembers and one who doesn't is, that the one who remembers is awake, and when you look into the eyes of someone who is awake, you feel touched to remember, because the person has evolved longer or evolved quicker. One time he didn't run. Instead of standing there shaking in his shoes, then running away, he stood there and shook in his shoes, then took a step forward. He dared to do so. It is always a choice, to accept or reject - to go forward or to move back or stand still. It is always a free choice, and the *one who remembers*, can encourage you forward but they cannot take that step for you. If you run away, you run away, but sooner or later you will be back. The only difficulty is, the longer you put it off, the more you live with that haunting melody of *Remember me.... Remember.....* The longer you feel lonely, the longer you feel sad."

Loving Crow: "To the awakened person who translates, (dies) the person who, in this lifetime, awakens to respond to the 'Remember me... who attains the Consciousness of the primordial teachings...... does this person reincarnate again? A very wordy question, but I don't know how else to ask....."

"That, too, is a matter of choice. It is always a matter of choice. Only before the awakening, it was not a conscious choice. After the awakening, it is a conscious choice and to come back is merely a choice of service to mankind. There could be no other reason to come back. You would already know how to *do* things in life... how to *present your dream* to express the God Force, so there could be no other reason to come back. You already have done everything, except in service, to help somebody else remember."

Kookaburra: "I have goose bumps on my arms from your words, 'Remember me.' How long does it take to remember?"

"In *a moment.... in a moment.... in a moment.* It doesn't have to drag on once you stop running. Remember, after you stop running, you have a moment of reverberation... the tremble period, and it is not a tremble from fear so much as it is of shock. Everything in your world, in your life, in your consciousness trembles at the shock from no longer running..... It feels like an earthquake. The earth trembles, then it stops. And, when it stops, it's new.... crossed over.

"You are beginning to remember. You are now trembling as you accept your remembering. Once you accept it, then the memories begin to flow. It takes tremendous courage, but the tremendous courage just takes seconds of action. Simplest is wholeheartedness.... standing still and saying, *'I've got to know. I'm going to do it.'* ...... Keep your eye on the bulls-eye... never off the bulls-eye....... Never, never, never take your eyes off the bulls-eye."

Kookaburra: "How do you release the little self?"

"The little self is your fantasy. It can be a long arduous struggle, or it can be just as quick as saying/doing, *'Release'.*...... Just Release.... Let Go...... As quickly as you can *let go*, it is done. It takes much evolvement to get to that point to be able to *let go*, because life begins with feelings of survival. In primitive life forms, a leech clings to things, afraid to let go, its entire life force is geared to hanging on, and as it evolves through the species.... through the bugs and the birds; and the birds are letting go, unraveling, pulling above, rising above, evolving......

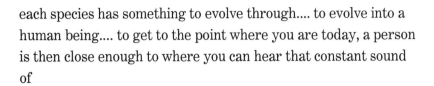

each species has something to evolve through.... to evolve into a human being.... to get to the point where you are today, a person is then close enough to where you can hear that constant sound of

'Remember me........."

Red Tail Circling: "Why don't we remember from one lifetime to the next?"

"Maybe you forgot from one incarnation to another, because you made a choice not to listen to the song of 'Remember me', but before that you were working up to it.

"You, as a part of the Void (God) broke away to get into a dreaming body, whether it be the simplest form of life or the more evolved. When you become a sentient being for the first time, it was the simplest form of life...... perhaps a slug. You were living as pure Soul without much consciousness, because the consciousness your body carries as a slug only knows it wants to survive......"

Loving Crow: "Do we 'experience' in the Void?"

"The Void is forever expanding. As you and I as a part of the Void, as Soul, learn to present and experience life through presentation, the God Force of the Void is expressed, and as that occurs, the Void evolves. You are **within** the Void *NOW*, as you would be if you were a conscious part of the Void. The difference is consciousness or unconsciousness, awake or asleep..... The Void is always becoming. There *is* no final movement.

"The Void is an ultimate force. It is an *evolving* ultimate force. It is always evolving. The Godhead - God, is not static, It

is *always* becoming...... *Always* becoming.... *Always*
becoming...... *Always* remembering.... *Always* remembering....
Always dreaming, remembering, dreaming, remembering....
becoming....... *Always* becoming......... **through service.** ....
Service is an expression of the dream force..... Always
becoming... Always is... Always is..... Always becoming... Always
becoming is.... I am that. **I am that I am**""'

Wolfsong: "Does compassion increase with each evolution?"

"Perhaps. The evolution of all things is heightened and made
more aware through your own awareness..... your own
wakefulness. All things are enlivened. We had times in the
wintertime when the ducks and the geese would gather around
here.... like they were listening.... trying to remember...... and, a
couple of rats sat near the door.... and the horses came over, and
they ate right in front of the Happy House."

Wolfsong: "Is awakening a state of consciousness?"

"It is consciousness, definitely, and you see, you and I are the
same.... You and I are one..... You and I are Soul.... Because I
remember that I am pure Soul...... Because I am aware and
awake to that fact.... when you look at me..... *you Remember
it*........

   "When you *Remember*, you can hear the teachings. When
you look at me and you resonate in that looking, you
remember...... You remember something about that look.... about
that togetherness.

   "At that moment, you are open enough to receive the
teachings...... And that opening gets greater and bigger each

time that you accept them. The more you can accept, the more you will remember.

"So, if you have a life of no resistance; if you are so completely open that no matter *what*, you are going to walk that impeccable line.... It is the only thing that matters.... the whole of whole, *of whole, of whole,* because you are the Void. You are That! And, you begin to remember It; so therefore, you know everything the Void is."

Kookaburra: "What does 'Higher Consciousness' mean?"

"Higher consciousness is an awareness of yourself as Soul, at which point, when you truly become aware of yourself as Soul, not from an intellectual concept but a true, alive awareness, you also, then recognize yourself as a part of God. This is the Higher Consciousness."

Kookaburra: "Are there degrees of Higher Consciousness' mean?"

"There are degrees or levels of awakening and, as you become more and more less resistant and more open, you automatically step inside.... closer..... closer.... closer.... closer.

"The Void is always becoming. I am always becoming. I am always becoming. You are always becoming, if you allow yourself to become.

"Once someone catches onto the fact that he can have this consciousness himself, his resistance will drop..... This is because the joy of *becoming* is greater than one's fear of it.

"May the blessings be."

The Path of Soul Aligns
Six Perfections

Generosity
Morality
Patience
Vigor
Sitting in the Silence
Wisdom

Winged Wolf: "The First, **Generosity**, is giving of yourself; at onement between yourself and all Life. It is sharing, not because you have to, or because there is any mental chatter to it, but because it is joyful to do. It is a state you come into where giving and sharing.... being generous, when somebody needs something from you, is not a task; but simply a privilege of the moment.

　Morality: When you are in tune as Soul, morality becomes a *natural state*, where you will not take advantage of other people, or situations; you will not covet other people's goods; you will not steal; you will not maim or kill with any pleasure. Now, sometimes you cannot help stepping on a bug, but you will not go around being obsessive about stepping on bugs. You cannot be obsessive about anything when you have true morality. You are simply free to live the teachings, and you will take each moment and decide what you want to do in that moment. Each moment presents new choices, and you base your decision on what you are experiencing in the moment, as Soul.

Patience: Give others a moment to collect themselves.... *to collect themselves* means that, as they come upon you, they may find there is a flutter within their personal environment, and that is because, you as Soul, have an *affect* on the people around you; give them a moment to adjust their senses to your presence. Wait *patiently* a moment, rather than to jump ahead, which would protrude into their space with your presence.

Vigor: As Soul, you naturally give wholeheartedly, 100% of yourself to whatever you are doing. *Real* vigor is your earnestness to whatever you are doing; you become One with *that.* Never hold back something once you have decided to do it or pull against yourself by saying, *you don't feel like doing it.* You either give, or you do not give, and if you are living as Soul, you are 100% with your choice in the moment.... this moment!

Sitting in the Silence: If you do not become comfortable in the silence, you will never be comfortable with yourself. There will always be restlessness.... always be restlessness.... always be restlessness without learning to sit in the silence. The more you have an urge to run this way or that way, the more you must learn to be still. When there is confusion and pandemonium going on around you, be still. Be absolutely still. Do not move a finger. Do not shift your eyes. Do not think in any direction.... Just Be Still. And if you cannot stop thinking, then at least do not move your body. By not moving your body, your mind will find a state of repose. It might take a little time, but it will find a repose.

Sitting in the Silence leads to the grand prize.... **wisdom.**

"All of these precepts fit together, and that really is what they are.... precepts for the person who wants to live as Soul. What one gains is wisdom. If you can keep your body still, the confusion in your life will resolve itself, and through that resolution, you will gain wisdom; you will know how to act; how to respond; how to speak to people; how to deal with situations; how to love; how to be a disciplinarian; how to be gentle; how to be harsh; you will learn *everything* you need to know. If you will learn to be quiet, then wisdom will be born in you.

"These are simple ways to live, and they have to be lived purely, not from a mental point of view. However, in the beginning, as you *sit in the silence*, and your mind runs in every direction, if you are able to keep your body still, gradually your mind comes under control. This methodology works the same way with all the precepts. If you *maintain morality;* if you *maintain* vigor; *if you can maintain your patience*; if you can do all these things through your own self-discipline; gradually, you will take them into a new order within yourself, where *sitting in the silence* will become natural.

"So you can begin this way by being wholehearted; by being generous.... But here is the thing.... If you act from a reactive point of view, it will get mixed-up inside of yourself. You will get caught up in mind chatter, as you are acting. *'Oh, I am doing this for so-and-so'*, because you are in a mental kind of a situation, whereby you break the precepts down into rationalizations, and when you do that, you are interfering, instead of adding to or assisting someone else. You are then not living as Soul, because to live as Soul is spontaneous, without rationalization.

"So, first of all, you must have self-discipline. When you become wholehearted, do not rationalize why you are being wholehearted, or why you are being generous, or why you are being moral. If you tell yourself you are being moral for some specific reason, then you are no more as Soul than when you were being immoral. This may be difficult to understand, but it is true, because the *mind passions* are set in motion when you rationalize why you are doing something. Rationalization puts you into a state of vanity; puts you into a state of attachment, do you see? When you judge things, you are living in a state that is borderline anger. This is very tricky, and that is why you cannot rationalize or mull over so much about what you are doing. You have to learn to make choices through *looking* at something to determine in energy if you want to go this way or that way. Whenever you get your mind chatter going, you activate your rational mind. And no matter how well you can rationalize an intention, no matter how honorable you may feel your intentions are, they are still *conjured* and *manipulative.*

"This is a very difficult Path, a very simple one; but a very difficult one, because you have to learn a new way of doing things. Suddenly, words take on a new meaning; you now have to accept the precepts and live them, without any kind of mental *mumble jumble* going on. This is tricky.... The key to finding clarity comes from *sitting in the silence,* because once you can *sit in the silence*, then you can access your *wisdom body.* The precepts are then easy; lack of rationalization becomes natural.

"So you have to revert to spiritual practices -- the singing of the HÜM, the *sitting in the silence,* and actively living life from the Third Eye.... It is better to practice simplicity, than to rationalize throughout your day about how to live the precepts. Simply practice walking through your life with your attention at the Third Eye. And because life may be stressful at times, because the environment may tug at you, you must also take the time to *sit in the silence....* to allow that which happened throughout the day to drop off of you. If you instead pile the chaos up around you and then go to bed, you will feel an agitation built around your body, and agitation is impatience. Impatience strikes anger in the environment, do you see? This is why *sitting in the silence* is always important - for one to allow what has been accumulated, to shed itself; then to walk about your day practicing your attention at the Third Eye. Do this and the other precepts will fall into place. It is as simple as that.

"Generosity + Morality + Patience + Vigor + Sitting in the Silence = Wisdom. Each is a quality of wisdom, and through wisdom, you will attain enlightenment. So there is always the *gold ring* waiting for you!

"Practice the aliveness of being as Soul.

"May the blessings be."

"Practice the Aliveness of Being as Soul."

Decision Making
(Finding and Choosing Gateways to Enhance One's Life)

Winged Wolf: "Making a simple decision oftentimes becomes a complex task. The complexity stems from fear of a condition(s) that could arise as a result of the direction that is taken: *"Where will such a decision lead me?" "Will the choice become a financial burden?" "Will it deter me from my goal?" "What effect will the decision have upon my family?" "In what way will my lifestyle change?"* These fears are understandable but unnecessary.

"The first thing a person must do is to decide what they want out of life. The goal need not be tangible but it should be realistic. 'Realistic' does not mean that it fits into the 'ordinary' scheme of life, as most people live it. Realistic means accepted as attainable by the individual setting the goal. If your goal is too large for you to accept, use the first step of that goal as your target and proceed towards that. When attained, move to the second step. When your vision expands enough to prove your destination to yourself, then return to the Big Picture.

"Next, take action. Once a decision is made it should immediately be followed by action. Most people make a decision and then sit around waiting for some impetus to occur to enforce motion in their lives. It does not work that way. In truth, this type of sitting around waiting for something to happen is procrastination. What usually happens when someone procrastinates is that they lose their moment in time; that is, the gateway or direction they saw before them when they made their decision, closes up. It may open again but it may be a long time. One of the most peculiar and interesting laws of life is, **Much makes More.** Have you ever noticed that, if you set your sights on looking for something, such as feathers, and you pick up the

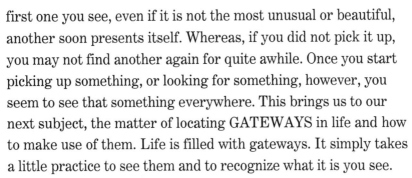

first one you see, even if it is not the most unusual or beautiful, another soon presents itself. Whereas, if you did not pick it up, you may not find another again for quite awhile. Once you start picking up something, or looking for something, however, you seem to see that something everywhere. This brings us to our next subject, the matter of locating GATEWAYS in life and how to make use of them. Life is filled with gateways. It simply takes a little practice to see them and to recognize what it is you see.

"Walk into a forest clearing. It can be a tiny meadow or clearing in a forest or even a small clearing in the center of a desert, a place where no brush grows. Become very quiet as you look around yourself. Draw your attention to the Third Eye at the center of your forehead and look out at what you see. Do this without mentally commenting at what you see. Simply LOOK. Notice that there is an opening between some trees or brush where you could comfortably walk through. It is not necessary to see what is beyond the opening, and there may be four or five around you, because the opening(s) are gateways and each gateway leads to another opening or gateway. Now here is the tricky part. With your attention at the Third Eye, because this is the place of the quiet mind, where there is no conflict, choose the most appealing gateway and go through it. Once you choose a direction, GO FOR IT.

"Walk through the chosen gateway and again, pause to look around. Is there another gateway in front of you that is appealing? Go through it as well. When you get to the other side, LOOK around. Where did it lead you? Did the passageway you followed present another gateway and is that gateway headed in a direction different than your original chosen directions?

"In this next clearing, notice if there is a hill. Set your sights on going toward and up the hill, choosing appealing gateways that will lead you there. Of course, you will want to continue this exercise with your attention on your Third eye, because you will NATURALLY choose a suitable gateway from this perspective. The Third Eye is the perspective of Soul. Soul always succeeds in its destination to a goal, and Soul always reaps positive abundance from its destiny. So you see, the Spiritual Warrior, one who lives as Soul, centered at the Third Eye, has a built in protection device.

"Once you become comfortable with practice sessions in nature, you will recognize their parallel with everyday life. Everyday life is filled with gateways, but, before choosing, it is wise to set a direction, destination or goal. After you have set your goal, you will have to monitor your impulse reactions to changing courses. If you are living as Soul, this next step will not concern you, however, for those less than adept at BEing as Soul, there is a way to know if you are on track, or OFF.

"In *The Flight of Winged Wolf*, my teacher Alana Spirit Changer uses a stick as an analogy to life. She explains that *'there are two ends to the stick. One is thought, mind, and the other end is consciousness or Soul.'* On the mind side are attitudes and opinions, passions and fears, intermingled with facts and facsimiles. The Soul end of the stick is cognizant of the mind side, sees it as a computer with both valuable and fraudulent information, and exercises wisdom in choosing from its data banks.

"Wisdom comes into play when there is a burning desire to go in a particular direction. This desire comes out of the blue, out of context and it can make you want to leave something behind you once very dearly wanted. This burning desire means that you are sitting in your seat of power and, because of fear of disappointment, or restlessness, wanting to give it up. When these feelings of passion present themselves, do not set goals or targets in front of you. Instead, sit still. Go to a movie or a ball game. Engage in some leisure time activity until your uneasiness subsides. Another safe rule of thumb is to wait four days before acting. If, after the fourth day, it still feels like the way for you to go, then LOOK for a gateway and proceed. Remember, like the exercise of choosing a gateway in nature, gateways to a goal in life have a glow and are attracting. Always approach them as Soul.

"May the blessings be."

"Once a decision is made it should immediately be followed by action."

Arenas of Clarity

Winged Wolf: "Once upon a time there was an apprentice who loved to read and learn new things. This apprentice always had her nose in a book and knew this fact and that fact. She knew all the facts about enlightenment; she had read all about how to get there. She knew about dreaming, and she knew about the Void and she felt she knew where other apprentices stood on the Path and everything else.... Every fact there was to know, she knew. She knew why the sky was blue. She knew why the grass was green. She knew.... she knew.... she knew....

"She was a knower of things! But there was one problem that she had: One fact got mixed up with another fact, and it was all stirred together in one pot. If you have ever cooked before, you know how it is.... you take a little of this and a little of that, and a little of this and a little of that, and a whole lot of this and a whole lot of that, and put it all together into the pot, and you know what? It tastes just like something you cannot possibly imagine.

"First of all, it looks kind of brown. And it may taste like that brown substance you may be imagining right now. The brown substance is actually the contents of her mind. (Laughter) You see?

"This morning I heard someone say, *'Oh, I understand that people who are enlightened don't unconsciously dream.'* And I said, *'That's right, it's a conscious dreaming.'* And she said, *'Well, I'm not going to dream anymore. Every time I start to dream, I'm going to stop myself and remind myself that enlightened people do not dream.'* I said, *'Well, let's put it aside for now and we'll talk about it this morning.'* (Laughter)

"Clarity cannot come from books. It can only come from experience with the teachings and this means you must integrate the teachings into your life. You become one with them. When you become one with the teachings, then you know they are no longer something from a book; they are a part of your life, a part of you.

"It is true that an enlightened person does not dream in the ordinary way in their sleep. This means they do not have symbolic type dreams. (Looking at Loving Crow), I said that to you before, but now you read it in some other books and you're taking it out of context to the teachings that have been given to you by me. I suggest that you put aside your books for a little while, all of you.

"Learn to be still inside, to be quiet. Learn what clarity is about. When you no longer have reverberations inside your brain to dictate how you should behave, or how you should not behave, then it will be all right to read again. But that might take many years because you have been stuffing things into your brain for a long time.

"Now, I'm not talking about education; facts are important. It is important to know some scientific facts; you know, about the roundness of the earth plane, (laughs) that kind of thing. It's important to know how to add 2 + 2. It's important to know how to read and comprehend, so that you can read contracts and be able to negotiate your way in the world. All of these things are important.

"But the type of learning you are talking about, (Looking at Loving Crow), is out of context with your teacher's guidance, and it is not important. All it does is make little detours, tiny roadways to constantly follow while you're trying to walk the path. And you are taking those detours or roads because you feel you are not going fast enough on the Path of Soul; when, in actuality you are moving quite fast, especially if you are concentrating on this Path.

"The Jeweled Path of Living as Soul is a path of action. You cannot participate in the action if your attention is always pulled off, onto side-trails. It slows down your movement on the Path itself, because you're off on side-trails, do you see? I want you to stay on the major thoroughfare. If you are my apprentice, you should work with me. Put aside your side-traits, not that all those teachings are not valid, they may be, but without the teacher they are just little bits and pieces, do you see?

"Milarepa didn't have to contend with much from his apprentices because there were very few books in those days. The writings were limited and it took a long time to get somewhere. If you have a teacher and yet you run down the road to visit somebody else as a teacher, and then down this other road again to visit somebody else as a teacher, what do you have? You receive little five minute snatches everywhere. But reading is even more deadly, because with those teachers at least you would be able to see where the teachers were coming from to decide what they meant. In picking up a book, you just get little written snatches, that's all. You create these little 'finger-ling' trails in your life and there can be no clarity that way. Without clarity, you cannot live the teachings.

"If you are a sincere student of the Path, then you give yourself to IT. And don't care if you are told not to read. You trust that. At some point, when you have clarity, you will pick up any book and automatically understand it. You may not care to read it at that point, do you see, because it's already a part of your life. Sometimes, you may. I pick up books and I read them in fifteen, twenty minutes and you will do that as well.

"So, put aside your restlessness, trying to get ahead of yourself and be where you are. Live this moment so wholeheartedly that it moves you to the next place in consciousness, because it will. You'll suddenly spill into that next arena.

"You know, the Path winds sometimes. Let's just say it's a long path straight out ahead of you and in certain areas it opens up into wide arenas and those are fields of learning.

"When you get into a journey (lesson), the words, themselves, of the journey sound familiar, because they are familiar. Also you are so accustomed to reading a book and saying, *'Oh, this is familiar,'* and then going over here and reading something else and saying, *'This is familiar.'*

"When I give you a lesson, I am asking you to live it... to be that... to accomplish that material. So when you come to those little arenas, stay in there and work with it, and when you accomplish it... when you accomplish that arena... when you become champion of that arena... not in contest with somebody else, but with yourself... when you become champion of that arena, then you can continue onto the next.

"There can't be any hurry to it. So, to frivolously say, *'I'm going to stop dreaming,'* to accomplish that, you would have to wake up all night. That would be kind of interesting to watch, we will have a crabby apprentice running around here. (Laughter)

"Dreaming, itself, stops as you reach a certain point, but you do not ever try to stop it. It stops in the ordinary way because you have begun to be aware of the process in your sleep. You wake up in the dream and, as you wake up, you choose those dreams very carefully. You do not participate in all those arenas. There is no confusion or conflict to the day, so there is nothing to symbolically work out.

"When there is clarity, there doesn't need to be an explanation. So you don't go to sleep to dream for an explanation of what you experienced the day before. There are types of dreams that go beyond that. And they will be dream experiences with your teacher, or maybe you will have an experience viewing the future from where you stand now. But bear in mind, those experiences about the future can change very quickly.

"One different turn in a day can change the whole picture, which is why a teacher watches an apprentice to see where they are going for a sustained period of time. You may be perfect today, can you be perfect tomorrow? You may have arrived in that new arena in this one place, do you see? Will something happen two minutes from now to throw you out of balance? When it becomes sustained, you are ready for the next step; not just when you grasp the material.

" *'Oh, I know this, I understand this.'* Good, live it and you will not care to rush, and then you are naturally moving on. Now, we are not speaking of an ordinary consciousness that is stuck, saying, *'I don't care if I move on.'* Someone on the Path of Soul is automatically an extraordinary consciousness.

"Someone who has worked off enough karma to walk the Path, is a big deal. You people have lived many, many lifetimes in preparation. There's still much to explore at -- but do not get caught up in textbooks --

"There are some people who go to school to get a Bachelor's degree, and then go after a Master's degree and then they get a Ph.D. - possibly they get another Ph.D. You know, they become students forever and they never do anything with it. They are scholars alone with not much clarity or understanding of what they are learning, because their knowledge only comes from textbooks.

"A true scholar will take his work out into life to validate it, and that is what you are doing on the Path of Soul. You are learning and validating, expanding and exploring. In this arena you become accomplished at what you want to be."

Loving Crow: "It appears to be such a dichotomy because in the books that I read, a lot of what I read is sitting, alone in meditation, yet, your teachings -- the teachings -- are not sitting, but living -- instead of hiding out on the mountain or something. It's a dichotomy; it's different."

"Hiding out on a mountain sounds lovely. Living life is also lovely. If you cannot live life according to your own dream energies, visions that you project out; if you cannot explore the mirror of your mind, which is life -- it's all rather useless. Anybody can sit still and not be disturbed, but there is that part of the practice, as well.

"Shamanism is active; it's not monastic. In the arena of life, it is a mirror image of your own mind. If you do not like what you see, you adjust yourself through your clarity. As you walk the Path of Soul, refinement is natural. You become what it is that you want to be, not through conjuring, not through visualization, just through being."

Loving Crow: "The very fact that it's simple, does not mean it's easy."

"It's very simple and it is very difficult, difficult only because of one's lack of clarity. Once the clarity sets in, it's simple and easy."

Loving Crow: "I was reading 'Through The Crystal,' (by Winged Wolf). It says that to have power, you must become the power. So, in my studies *on the Path with you, the above statement means that to live as Soul, you have to become that. Well, how do you become **that** which is the power to live as Soul? How do you do that? Just go journey after journey after journey.... I mean it's like -- just be! It's not..."*

"It is just being, however, one must cultivate the soil for something to grow."

Loving Crow: "There you go!"

"You have to shed the baggage that you have been carrying. You have to pull the weeds and sweep off the dead leaves or mulch them into the soil. There is preparation. If you have done your preparation and you have come into this lifetime with all your preparation done, it's a boon! (pause) That's very rare! Perhaps next lifetime."

Loving Crow: "It could be this lifetime if I prepare... stay in those arenas."

"No, I meant to be born into it. I have no doubt you will do it this lifetime, if you stay focused."

Loving Crow: "Thank you!"

Wings of Change: "To keep from making those detours, it's really important to have your teacher, isn't it, because without that, I'm still in my myth."

"Yes, you are just making 'finger-lings,' but remember, your teacher had a teacher as well. I did not come into this lifetime free, I knew many things, but my freedom had to be unearthed, like digging up a buried treasure."

Wolfsong: "What does that mean?""

"It means that I knew as a child what I know now, but I could not live it, because I needed the companion energy of somebody else (a teacher) to agree with what I knew. The world was contrary to what I knew. My family said the opposite from what I knew; religions said the opposite and schools said the opposite. Mr. X kept saying, *'Yes, yes, you've got it.'* And then came a long dark period when he wasn't there and I floundered around feeling lost and alone. And then Alana made me remember to live what I knew. I already knew it. I knew it when I wrote *The Sedona Trilogy.*"

Loving Crow: "It was all there!"

"It was all there. But I didn't have any validation, I only had my own voice coming back at me or a voice from the teacher that I didn't see too often, Mr. X."

Wings of Change: "But when you have validation, something bigger occurs."

"Yes! Companion energy -- nothing exists without it. Without the companion energy, you cannot move forward. We are not singular beings. Milarepa had Marpa."

Loving Crow: (faint voice) "And we have you."

"Uh-huh, but only because I had my teachers."

Loving Crow: (faint voice) "The knowledge of that validation."

"I remember once in one of my darkest times, I was caught up in all kinds of emotional stuff, because I was so lonely -- that loneliness of having no validation. And I was eating lunch from the work place out by a stream and I saw Mr. X move across a field. He waved to me and I ran after him.

"Mr. X did not talk to me, but his presence reminded me that I did not need to do what I had been doing and so I ended that chapter -- that little 'finger-ling' that was a big detour in my life at that time. Whenever I got really far out, I could always count on him.

"And then came the time in my life where I knew everything and did not have that validation friend. I was crying out inside of myself, 'If only I had a teacher that was mine -- a teacher for me -- somebody I could talk to, look at -- not up on a stage somewhere, you know, not with a telescope trying to see from a long distance -- but somebody I could interact with. And then I inherited a property in Colorado. I drove up there and went into a grocery store. When I came out, (laughs) I found this Indian woman, a Shaman, in my jeep.

"But even though I had wanted that, I didn't accept her for a long time, but Mr. X never appeared during that time. (pause) Just once I wanted him to come and say, 'You're doing it right!' you know."

Apprentices speaking in unison: "Validation!" (Laughter)

"Alana was my validation. (long pause) Cherish your path, honor it by staying out of the 'finger-lings' as much as you can and if you get caught up in some of them, well, remember that you made

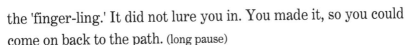

the 'finger-ling.' It did not lure you in. You made it, so you could come on back to the path. (long pause)

   "You know, up around that same place where I saw Mr. X at lunch-time, not too far up there, along the side of a river, I rented this clap-board cottage, just because I figured if I hung out there enough, I would see him again, and he would come and visit me. But he didn't, and I spent much time out there, hanging out by the river so that was good. It kept me out of 'finger-lings'. I kept my eye on the bulls-eye. (long pause) Keep your eye on the bulls-eye!

   "May the blessings be."

"*A true scholar will take his work out into life to validate it, and that is what you are doing on the Path of Soul ~ learning and validating, expanding and exploring.*"

One's Degree of Viewpoint
....A Picture of Life

Winged Wolf: "To recognize reality, it is important to recognize fantasy so that we can see how fantasy entraps an individual. When a person builds his/her life in companion energy with others, a spouse, children, and friends, and most intensely with those he shares living quarters with, he builds a fantasy as a viewpoint through which his life is viewed.

"This viewpoint is carried around with him; it is how he sees things; it is the place where his attitudes and opinions are formed. A person can go through their entire life without shifting viewpoints, but when there is a shift, it often comes about as a result of intense analysis that spells out a multitude of reasons and rationalizations with continued reluctance. So, as we see from all of this, the endangered viewpoint has greatly upset the life of the person, because his viewpoint constitutes the foundation of his life.

"Living your life from a set viewpoint is frequently called *stability* by people of like mind. It is very important to many people to live a stable, single-pointed life so that they can develop continuity in their lives, however they restrict the meaning of continuity to an overview of a single degree out of the 360 possible degrees.

"Most people live their lives from a one-degree viewpoint, and here is the difficulty. One person will see from a one-degree viewpoint from one degree that is, say, the 19th degree on the 360 degree wheel, do you see? And somebody else is over here at 27 degrees and someone else is at 56 degrees and somebody else at 72 degrees and 185 degrees or 285 degrees, do you see? Any single degree viewpoint is limited to that point of view, however, when an individual steps onto the Path of Soul, his or her personal myth begins to lose substance and rigid attitudes and opinions begin to drop away. When this happens, he or she begins to see more clearly from other viewpoint degrees, combining those previously traveled, and gradually combines the next level of unexplored viewpoints ahead. In other words, when someone who has been living from the 78th degree viewpoint, begins to reach out of his world, his visibility expands to incorporate viewpoints from 1 to 78 degrees, as well as those beyond where he sits. It is this freeing up process that begins the cycle that awakens a person to his spirituality.

"As a person gets beyond the one-quarter mark of 91.25 degrees of the whole 360, something happens. That person becomes at odds with the restrictive minds with people in the first quarter, and those in the first quarter see him as a rebel, a little strange and odd for them to be comfortable with. Those who see life from beyond the second-quarter or beyond 182.50 degrees on the 360 degree wheel also appear a little strange and weird, (laughter), to those in their first-quarter, and those in the second quarter. While people in the third-quarter of the 360 degrees, beyond the 273.75 degree viewpoint, are considered awesome. Their ideas often seem ingenious but impractical and such people are considered not in tune with the rest of the world. Some call them mad, but since they are very much in control of their lives, above being victims, more often they are referred to as visionaries, philosophers or so-called *egg-heads.* Such names relate to their ability to see great distances, only their far-sighted visions are usually mistrusted and scrutinized.

"Those beyond the third-quadrant in viewpoint see so vastly that they have the wisdom to temper their appearance to others. Within these final degrees of the 360 degree wheel of viewpoint, the individual grasps the significance of life and has already begun the homestretch to live as Soul. They have recognized God as the overview viewpoint that has the ability to grasp everything and anything, and their preparation has begun to *realize* the identity of God.

"Fantasies vary from the first quarter of the 360 degree viewpoint circle to the second and third quarters. The fantasies interact between these levels in unison with the nature of the fantasies. Friendly, social fantasies are more easy to swallow. The fantasy of an orchestra conductor has a sensitive, artistic fantasy (myth) that charms and arouses curiosity. The conductor may live in the third quadrant but he is accepted and respected by all because of the dignity and intelligence he portrays. Teachers, artists, doctors, and other professional people usually are accepted in this way as well. Their fantasies give sparkle to the fantasies in the first, second and third quadrants. Actually, it is the third quadrant people who lead the first two quadrants forward on the wheel of degrees. Their fantasies arouse curiosity and entice them forward.

"Those in the first and second quadrants have the tendency to be tightlipped with square, boxed-in ideas that are often rigid and hypocritical. They might be viewing their religion in a critical way because they do not like their priest, putting their dislike of a personality before the teaching itself.

"When a person in the first and second quadrant loses their support system, he is lost, because those who helped hold his views in place no longer exist. Naturally, he wanders into a strange environment and sees all these people in a different environment and they might be in different parts of a quadrant. Some of them might be in quadrant number one, but because they are at different degrees in that quadrant, he has not met them before, therefore, he can only see a part of them, the part that is a common denominator. Because there seems to be so many blind spots, he feels conflict and constant discomfort.

"So the person who is in quadrant number one with this constant discomfort with *outsiders* taking care of him, feels so out of sync with them, that he starts fighting. He gets angry, *'I'm not understood.'* And then he begins to think to himself, as he watches those in these different viewpoint degrees, and says, *'Okay, I know what this person's doing. I'm going to pretend that I'm in companion energy.'* Then he pretends a game for this person and he pretends a game for that person, and so on, only he cannot keep his pretense (lies) straight because he is hanging onto his attitudes and opinions from quadrant number one. Do you see? The pretender knows what he is doing, but in a way he does not know either. Mostly he is mimicking some behavior he sees, but does not understand the behavior, so it gets kind of intense and mixed-up.

"A person cannot maintain his viewpoint without the companion energy of another and there can be no companion energy in pretense. In quadrant number one, you are totally dependent on somebody to support that position. Respect or genuineness cannot be pretentious. In quadrant number one, you have a very narrow field to choose from. From that place in consciousness, all people of another religion are not so good, and people of another race are not so good either. You see? To them you have to be a certain thing in order to be accepted. To many of that like-mind, you cannot be divorced. However, they will change their view if their child divorces, but not anybody else. To them, their child had extenuating circumstances.

"So here they are out there without any support and their world is totally unstable. How can you help somebody like that? You cannot! Because if you try to enter their world at any degree, they know that you are not a part of it, do you see? That much they do know. They do know that you do not live from their viewpoint, so they think you're pretending, so they pretend, and their pretense gets very complicated.

"They look at something and they interpret it and they interpret it from their one percent viewpoint, wherever it is in that first quadrant, or second or third quadrant. But you see, the latter quadrants are not as limited because they have a greater vision. The fourth quadrant, because it reaches into the viewpoint of the whole, is exempt from this discussion, whereas the third quadrant is still trapped in the dual worlds of pro and con, black and white, etc..

"In that first quadrant, vision is so limited, there is only a little tiny sliver of light. (Winged Wolf uses her hands to show a small sliver.) And then in degree number two there is a little bit more and then it widens and widens and widens. So one's field of vision can be very narrow, and the more narrow, the more frightening it is.

"May the blessings be."

> "*A person cannot maintain his viewpoint without the companion energy of another, and there can be no companion energy in pretense.*"

Mind Passions

Winged Wolf: "We are going to talk about mind passions, or what other people call emotions. You see, emotions assume various forms of mind passions, which is why a person's emotional body can never be healed. It can only be transcended. Please listen carefully as we discuss the nature of mind passions.

"The first one we will take a look at is *lust.* Lust comes in other forms than sex. Lust comes in the form of an insatiable hunger, an insatiable hunger for anything - an insatiable hunger for success; an insatiable hunger for *more* of something.

"*Vanity* overlaps lust, as all the mind passions do. Each emotion overlaps the other emotion. There is not one emotion that stands totally by itself. They all are really one, just like all the Soul attributes are *one*. Vanity can take the form of, *'I'm better than somebody else',* or *'I am less than somebody else.'* It can go either way. Vanity can say, *'I am not worthy',* or vanity can say, *'I should have.'* You see, when somebody feels they are unworthy, it is because their *little self* or their ego is coming into play, saying, *'I am not worthy of this',* which is ego with another face. It is staring at the little self, because there should be no question since each of you, as Soul, are worthy of everything. Vanity takes precedence over feelings about what other people do. It passes judgment and scrutinizes, and says, *'Does this person measure up to this standard versus this standard, versus this standard'.* Well the truth of the matter is, if you are looking at someone with a critical eye, you are seeing them (scrutinizing) through the eyes of your myth, so what you see is your own myth coming back at you. If you are seeing someone as Soul, then you would see their bits and pieces quite differently, and there really would be no judgment attached to it - you would be just *seeing*.

"Vanity scrutinizes, trying to get one to measure up to your standards. And you know what? Unless you can truly pass judgment on yourself, you cannot really pass judgment on the other person, because you are the measuring device. So, it doesn't work out really well.

"*Greed*.... Like lust, greed is a desire for more and more of something. There is never enough. Greed is born from a fear of loss. When you are afraid you are going to lose something, if you are afraid of loss, then you are greedy; you see, because you can't really lose anything. If something is important to your life, you might *drop* it. For example, I was walking along and I had some ice cleats that I had sent off for from a magazine, and this morning (in the snow) I thought, *'Oh well, now I get to try these out.'* So, I pulled them over my boots. Later while I was walking up the road with them on, (when you pivot on your foot, automatically the rubber cleat pops off), I suddenly recognized that one of them wasn't on my boot and doubled back to get it. So, that is losing something but not really, and even if I had lost it, it would not have been a loss, you see. It was a very limited little gadget, not made well. So, that kind of loss isn't anything.

"You really can't lose anything that is yours, because there isn't any such thing as loss. But greed says, *'I must not lose. I cannot afford to have loss. I have to worry about this, that, or the other thing.'*

"I have spoken to you about *attachment* many times. Attachment is greed, and it is vanity, and it is lust, and it is anger because, if you are attached to something, you fear you are going to lose it, and you become very angry. It is very upsetting and you become frustrated, and when you are frustrated, you are *angry,* another mind passion or poison.... When you are depressed you are angry. That is why I ask that you clarify the meaning of your words. If you say you are depressed, you are angry. Maybe you are not talking about your anger, but it is stirring around inside of you.

"Now, these mind passions are always sitting around. They are like what a negative is to a photograph. They are always there. They don't go anywhere. They only come forward when a conditioned response is pushed in you; in other words, when some little button you have set in your brain brings a *passion* forward.

"Sustained anger is poison. If you are angry for more than three seconds, and I will say this one million times until everybody gets it.... you have three seconds to drop it! You have fifteen seconds to drop any other mind passion in any form, otherwise, you are going to have its effect in your life that you will have to live out. Winged Wolf softly says, *'Be Careful. Be Careful. Be Careful.'*

There is a very long pause followed by Winged Wolf saying, "Shhh." Energy from some of the apprentices in the Happy House is bouncing in all directions. She directs those seated to focus on a figure that is woven into the pattern on the rug....

"See that little figure in the center. Not this figure (she points to a form that looks like a monkey) the second figure that is kind of faint? Apprentices nod, affirming the form on which she is directing attention. Without trying to decide what it is or is not, I would like for you to just look at him, and keep your attention there so that you can focus on what I am saying because, when your mind gets busy, it is like trying to be heard in a crowded room.... you are racing ahead, thinking about this, that, and the other thing of what we were talking about.... you do not need to do that. All you need to do is to listen. If you listen, I can talk to you. (Again a long pause.)

"So then we have a general idea of what the mind passions or emotions are. If someone says something to you and it brings a rise in you, the rise is usually emotional. Emotions rise and fall within you. That is all they are.... rises and falls. They spring up and they go down. They spring up and they go right down. If you feel something start to spring up, just let it alone, or switch it off, and when you get so that you are really good at that, then you are not going to have it rise up as often. Gradually, the *rising up* will fade away.

"Your emotions never really serve you, except when you use a mocked up expression. You can use a loud voice or a sharp tongue if somebody cannot hear a soft voice, and you know, there are people who cannot hear soft voices. The reason they cannot hear soft voices, is that they have been listening to harsh ones for so long, they cannot hear when spoken to softly. If you don't use a sharp tone with them, then they do not understand what you are saying.... they don't even hear what you are saying. They are talking in their minds at the same time you are talking to them, so this is why each apprentice is treated differently. It is much more fun when someone can be treated with a soft tongue, but sometimes you have to use a loud voice.... put a growl into your voice, only don't allow yourself to feel it in your solar plexus while you are doing it. If you are feeling it in solar plexus, then you know it is no longer mocked up. You have gotten hooked into it, so let that go.

"Anytime you feel yourself getting hooked by getting caught up in passing judgment on a person, you should know you are caught up in the mind passions of *anger, lust,* and *vanity,* and you are *attached* to those feelings, so you are experiencing *attachment* as well. You see, the mind passions really overlap from one to the other.

"This is a practical discussion to help you *let go* of whatever is bothering you. If you need to make an overt expression to someone, let it rise, *'Hey, cut that out!'*, and then go on to something else. Make someone shiver in their shoes a little bit, and right now my voice (referring to just raising her voice) didn't mean a thing. You see, it is just right back to normal again.... So, that is just a mocked up use of.... I don't want to say emotion because it is not really an emotion.... It is not really felt. An emotion is something that is stirred from the pit of your solar plexus, and rises out of you in a torrent. If it is a silent torrent, it is depression.

"Parents need to talk sharply to their children once in awhile. In business, if someone is not listening to you, and you are trying to get a point across, you have to stand firm, and use a firm voice so that you will be heard. Winged Wolf sternly says, *'I cannot accept your proposal.'* Do you see? The sternness is a tool that is not *felt* in you; it is, however, a proclamation to the other individual to pay attention to what it is you are trying to get across. Maybe their mind is so busy, all that is being heard is their own mental chatter, and you are trying to get a point across. Because you are in the middle of a negotiation, it has to be a WIN-WIN situation; otherwise, it is no good. If only you win, and the other person loses; well, you do not have a negotiation. If the other person is winning and you are losing, you do not have a negotiation there either. It has to be WIN-WIN. A negotiation has to serve the whole, and if an individual is not paying attention to the needs of the whole, then you are going to have to get their attention, because you are a part of that whole, do you see? But, do not get the energy you project hooked into your solar plexus. Do not get a knot forming inside of you, where you feel you are going to burst with anxiety inside of yourself. Instead allow yourself to rise up and speak in the strongest voice necessary, and then in the next instant, be gentle. Again, Winged Wolf speaks very harshly and loud, *'Please listen to me.'* (and then softens). Do you see how quick I am to go back and forth? You can smile while you are doing this. Practice so that you will not feel contrived while speaking up.

"If you allow your *speaking up* time to pass; and somebody is telling you something and you are not speaking up because you do not want to upset them, you will begin to feel a little shaking feeling inside your solar plexus.... a little up and down shaky feeling. *'Oh, I'm not speaking up. I can't say anything'*, and all the while, you are shaking inside. Now, because you have not allowed yourself to respond to what is going on, you have allowed your solar plexus to become engaged, which means you must speak or it will eat at you for hours to come. You must not, however, speak in anger, so be careful. Realize you have built tension in your solar plexus area of your body, that your body, as a sensory machine is disturbed. When you feel a strong vibration in your solar plexus, you have stuffed something in there. So then you say, *'I am sorry but I cannot agree with what you are saying... etc.'* Let it out and then let it go, right away. Immediately, let it go! It is best not to get to that point where your feelings are stuffed inside of you. Although sometimes you may be in a group situation, when you feel that rattling-sensation in your solar plexus, you need to speak. This feeling usually occurs out of great principle, making you feel you need to speak, so do so.

"You can live a life that has power.... I do not mean pushing or pulling kind of power, I mean the power of wholeheartedness, a passion for your direction in life. You know, I am a passionate person in the way that I live the Path of Soul. In order to have the Path of Soul 100% in your life, you have to romance it. You have to love it. So, to love the Path of Soul takes a passionate nature, but the passion does not consume you at your solar plexus area.... nor does it turn on intrusive psychic energies, do you see? It is not that type of passion. It is a passion whereby things are *okay*. There is a very fine line between what you consider *okay* and emotions. There is really nothing okay about emotions. This is why you have to be very careful so that, when you use passionate expression, it comes from Soul Vision.

Dragonfly: *"It is the **doing** that is difficult."*

"The doing of what? Why don't you give me a for instance?"

Dragonfly: *"For instance, at work if someone is acting in a way that is not going to bring a win-win situation, because I am always trying to adjust my expectations so that we can both win, but if the other person is really adamant about something like a situation that happened two weeks ago. I was trying to explain to a person why I felt as I did, and she didn't even hear it. It was like, 'This is the way I am. I don't even hear it.' She didn't say that, but that is what I was receiving."*

"So, she was shaking at the solar plexus, throwing that out at you.... At that point, the best thing that you can do is take your hand and put it over your solar plexus and smile at her, excuse yourself and walk away, do you see? Or sit down to do your business or whatever, and just say, *'Well perhaps we should discuss it later.'* When you put your hand (either hand) over your solar plexus, you block the other person's energy from entering you."

Dragonfly: "I didn't do that."

"You see, if you get wrapped up in her emotion, then you both lost; it doesn't serve her anymore than it serves you. I say it does not serve her to come out on top in that way, because you will be unhappy and it will show in your continued work together. That kind of winning never does serve. It is too lopsided. So you could have said, *'Perhaps we should discuss this later'*, and then smile and walk away. She does not know what you are doing. Just put your hand over your solar plexus to protect yourself from her intrusive energies.

"May the blessings be."

"If you allow your speaking up time to pass; and somebody is telling you something and you are not speaking up because you do not want to upset them, you will begin to feel a little shaking feeling inside your solar plexus...."

Mind Passions or Mind Poisons

Anger
(Fear Motivated)

Rage, frustration impatience, resentment , bitterness, revenge, indignation, hostility, depression.

Lust
(Fear Motivated)

Obsessiveness, covetousness, unrestrained craving, over-indulgence, insatiable hunger.

Greed
(Fear Motivated)

Gluttony, self-absorption, possessiveness, jealousy.

Vanity
(Fear Motivated)

Conceit, insincerity, self-centeredness, self-importance, excessive pride in appearance or accomplishments.

Attachment
(Fear Motivated)

Possessiveness, deprivation, prolonged grief, control-centered, living in the past or in the future, inflexibility.

Living a Life of Power
Integrating the Teachings Into Your Life

Winged Wolf: "When I was an apprentice, my teacher Alana Spirit Changer frequently reminded me that 'knowledge learned off of the path' or 'knowledge without **do** (without action) was not valid.' If you cannot live what you know, then what good is all your knowledge," she would say.

"To <u>not</u> live what you know is a schizophrenic state of mind; that is, you are thinking one thing and living another. If you think you want to be an artist, and you daydream about it in a way that your beliefs see your world in that way, but you do not exercise your artistic abilities, you are living against your nature. Likewise, if you fantasize wanting to be a doctor and you are a merchant, you are living against yourself. Your actions are not lined up with your dreams or mental imagery, which is, according to shamanism, a schizophrenic condition.

"Living half-heartedly, or thinking one thing and doing another, brings about a half-hearted existence, one that results in discontentment, anger and drudgery. It is also the role of one who seeks but never finds.... The dreamer who visualizes what they want but never gets what they visualize.

"Shamanism asks that you put visualization techniques aside and, instead, teaches integration. The shamanic law of life affirms that, whatever it is you learn must also become a part of your moment to moment life. The realization that naturally follows this law is that you will have to assume responsibility for yourself - for every thought you have and every action you do or do not take. In other words, the excuse for non-performance can no longer be that you are a 'victim of circumstances'. Living your power means giving up your victim role in life, accepting that whatever happens is a direct result of your attention, via your choices and the consciousness you carry to produce your choices. As you move along the Path of Soul, living as Soul, a refinement process takes place.

"The teachings are primordial truths, first (known) recorded in a Country called Oddiyana, and later translated into Tibetan in a time-period that was pre-Buddhist. The teachings themselves are remnants of another yuga or cultural millennium now lost to the surface of our planet. The role of the teacher of these primordial truths was, and always has been, to guide the seeker into the remarkable core of this pristine science of existence, so that the seeker can acquire the necessary tools to facilitate a vision that can penetrate the illusions of mind-invented life. Mind-invented here refers to the fantasy(s) that occurs when mind images are produced through mental (or brain) stimulus. The clarity of the vision gained makes it possible, with the teacher's guidance, to recognize and shed one's personal mental baggage, and to align one's actions with one's dreams.

"Once an individual becomes free from unnecessary mental baggage and conscious of the dreaming mechanisms guarded by the sensory body, a remarkable intelligence occurs. The primordial part of the individual, Soul, takes command of one's brain, and their intelligence, memory and health is then greatly heightened. Once this occurs, a natural refinement takes place and the individual lives from the seat of divine love, compassion, joy and freedom.

"The teachings will begin to resonate in your sensory body, and begin to awaken ancient truths so penetrating to us all. They are clear and pure teachings.

"May the blessings be."

"Living your power means giving up your victim role in life, accepting that whatever happens is a direct result of your attention, via your choices and the consciousness you carry to produce your choices."

Movement

(Wolfsong comments that she was watching the smoke from the incense as it curled out from the stick and moved through the room eventually dissipating and wondering about the movement of things in life).

Winged Wolf: "Movement occurs through energy ties, and such energy ties do not have to be connected to a person or to a place. They can be fastened to another energy, as you witnessed this morning, sitting and watching the incense curl above its burner and then snake through the room. The patterns fascinated you and you wondered where they came from or how they came about."

Wolfsong: "Yes, I did."

"The incense united with a pattern of atoms and molecules that were already existent in the room. The patterns of energy (atoms and molecules) were formed and stirred into traveling a certain way by the movement of our human energy - thoughts, feelings, and breath, which is calmed or heightened by lack of thought, or thoughts and feelings. As you wonder something, the energy is propelled into motion; when you become silent inside, it rests without movement.

"So, unlike the atoms and molecules that are mostly invisible, the incense is a fluid visible matter that attaches to the winding roadway of invisible energy. People's perfume and colognes do this as well, and so do strong emotions. You may be walking down the street when suddenly, unconsciously, you will bump into a scent, or a feeling. It will either be pleasant or unpleasant. You know, a glob of atoms and molecules are left hanging in space by another person who recently passed through the area. So this is a good reason to be conscious and aware; a good reason to be present in the moment, so that you are not victimized by such energy. It happens to people all the time. Everything is going well until they enter a coffee shop, somehouse's house, an office building or step outside into the open air. However, globs of energy and/or scents outdoors do not linger long until they are resident there. There is one bayside corner on the island I live on that always smells like hot dogs. Indoor settings carry left behind energy for a longer period of time. Some very old buildings carry an accumulation of energy. Some strong influences will stick to the plaster or old wallpaper under the plaster, as they frequently do with antiques of any kind. You may go into a store and pick up an antique to look at, when you are hit by an unusual sensation. The energy of the sensation comes from the object and from you, what you were feeling in mood when you placed it between your hands. You may want to possess it or you may want nothing to do with it. If you are deeply conscious of what you are doing, as an experiment, you will observe such sensations without being affected. One day you may stroll down the street, deeply in engrossed in a happy thought, 'De,de,de,de....' and a short distance behind you somebody else bumps into your good feeling. 'Uh, what was that I felt? Oh, I just had a sensation. Ooh, where did that come from? How mystical,' (laughter) and it was just your sweet little pile of stuff that you left behind.

"You see how powerful you are, and this is why I tell you to contain your energy. Contain your energy, because what you put out there attaches somewhere, somehow. You may walk down an entire street and nothing attaches, but very likely, especially in a city or place where there are many people, something always attaches. You may walk down one street and nothing attaches, but when you go into a store, or when you return home whatever feeling was left behind will attach.

"So, you might be feeling really wonderful and then meet somebody as you are walking into your house who might have had a very bad day; however there is something in that intensity from their bad day that matches the intensity of your good day and you might walk into the room and suddenly, they are uplifted by your feelings. Of course, it can work the other way as well. You know, you can be pulled into their bad day. So the best way to live is with your energy contained. If your energy is contained, then you are not easily victimized, see?

"This is one reason spiritual adepts usually live privately in the mountains, the forest or by the sea. The stress level is greatly reduced, which is more compatible for the spiritual life. Between the Wind is such a place, a forest place by the sea, but having apprentices as visitors often alters the peacefulness. As I sit here with you, I make myself vulnerable so that I can tap into what is going on with you; so that I can guide you in your spiritual practices. You know, I can say, *'Okay, my body says....cough, cough.... somebody's energy over here is intrusive.'* So I say, 'Contain your *energy!'....* Then everybody snaps to.

"By my interaction with you, you become aware of what you put out; of what comes out of you. And you can see that your energy has an effect, and you know, even though you are doing it unconsciously with no ill intent, you are still responsible for it. If you throw a rock and it kills or injures someone, even though you did not mean to do so, you are responsible. If a child breaks a neighbor's window with a baseball, he is responsible for the broken window. If a boat speeds into a harbor and the wake from his boat upturns a kayak, he is responsible. Likewise, whatever energy you put out, you are responsible for. So if you are in a bad mood and your being in a bad mood affects somebody else, you will be held karmically responsible, even though the other person is responsible for himself; because, ultimately, everything is self-originated.

"Your body is a container for your energy. If your energy is contained as you go through life, you will be uplifting others. Even though you see somebody having a bad day or a rough time, if you cannot do something to help them, because that person does not want help, at least you can walk past him and not be injured. So life becomes pretty wonderful with your energy contained.

"If your energy is contained, you are centered at the Third Eye, which means that you have wisdom and therefore you can do anything. You can go anywhere, aware of the energy that is out there and make a conscious choice not to participate in it. *'I don't feel like I want to walk through all that junk that's going out there,'* you see? *'I'm going to go this way instead. Or maybe today I'm going to stay home. It's too intense out there. I don't care to even walk through it.'* Make your choices consciously, but the only way you can choose consciously is through containing your energy, and containing your energy results from being in Soul Vision.

"Now, here is a vitally important principle. Movement is connected to movement.... is connected to movement.... is connected to movement.... is connected to movement.... is connected to movement.... is connected to movement.... is connected to movement, and so on. If you make a conscious choice not to participate in the movement, you intercept it or you break the link in the chain. You know, those atoms and molecules that you left dangling out on the street.... well, somebody bumped into them, and they picked them up and they took them on to the next place that they went to. Your stuff affected them and they took it with them, and then as they are talking to somebody else, and that person felt those things that he had picked up from you and some of it rubbed off. Maybe it wasn't so great as the first time, or maybe it was even greater because maybe this other person was having a real bummer of a day. So, the negative stuff that you brought with you really became magnified on them. Do you see how this works?

"Some of you like to play energy games with others. If you have a game going with somebody, then you may be throwing a little cynical ball of energy back and forth that is growing in size. Such a game is warped or distorted by what each person identifies with karmically, your differences.

"So as you see the incense move through the room and it's taking dips and turns and twirls, it's connecting to little balls of energy that are already hanging out there, and that's how you do with your life. You make connections to like energy as you move through your day. If you do it in a contained way, in a responsible contained way, then you can see those energy blobs out there and you can make a conscious choice to connect with them or not to connect with them."

Loving Crow: "How do you sustain that awareness? You say that when you contain your energy there's an awareness of... How do you sustain that?"

"You mean aside from staying at the Third Eye?"

Loving Crow: "Yes. How do you sustain that awareness and/or how do you sustain being at the Third Eye?"

"Through being conscious. You have to be conscious when you're walking down the street of what you see, hear, smell, touch. You are aware of what your senses tell you. You cannot drift away in thought somewhere else, when you are going down this street down here. You must be present to the moment at hand. Being present mean you cannot be mentally wandering off, wondering about something that you need to do tomorrow, or what you did yesterday. You have to be here now. If you are totally conscious of the present moment, you are in Soul Vision. Align your actions with your dreams. You align your body with your mental imagery, living the imagery of your mind, of what your senses tell you."

Wings of Change: "If you're conscious enough to know that you've left that energy behind, is there a way to clean it up once that ball has been set in motion?"

"You mean rather than just having it karmically backfire. Yes. Through your awareness. Herein lies the strength of awareness. The power of awareness is incredible. You know, the perfume of incense is wandering in the room, attaching and going this way and that way. As soon as you become conscious of its movement, you can detach its energy, just through being conscious, not through saying *'Oh, now I'm going to reach over here and detach something,'* or to manipulate the energy this way or this way, but simply through your awareness lined up as Soul. It is eliminated from your mind images at this point and therefore dissipates.
   "May the blessings be."

"If your energy is contained, you are centered at the Third Eye, which means that you have wisdom and therefore you can do anything."

Transcendental Mind Energy

How the Mind Operates

Winged Wolf: "The location of one's mind in the body has been the source of puzzlement for philosophical thinkers from the beginning of time. The reason behind the parallax is that no one seems to know what the mind is or where it comes from. It is illusive, because when considered in intellectual thought, the mind naturally eludes description. Here is why.

"The brain is a computer-like mechanism that is programmed from birth by personal experiences - influences from one's past lives and karmic influences from this life, enlarged upon by one's parents, relatives, siblings, friends, educators, religion and society at-large. All of these influences establish or set programs within an individual's brain to produce reactions of a like (or similar) nature. Oftentimes these reactions are fear based, reactive triggers pulled to protect or to preserve one's ego. In other words, the brain is at rest until challenged by some occurrence with another individual, or from the environment - a loud or soft sound, or a visual sight of some kind, or a communication from another person - when, suddenly the brain sends off a blast of electrical energy.

"If you are right-handed, the electrical energy response begins on the left side of the brain; if you are left-handed, the response begins on the right side of the brain. Wherever this charge of electrical current originates on one side of the brain, it builds in energy until, like a lightning bolt bursting through a stormy sky, the current connects with the circuitry on the other side of the brain. Out of this electrical interaction or lightning-like current, the two sides of the brain are connected and there comes a sudden projection of electrical energy that then arranges or rearranges one's internal molecular structure, which projects an image seen by the internal eyes or what we call imagination, and finally, by the physical eyes, which gazes into the environment produced by the internal eyes. This is the image-making process, which results from the process brought about by brain stimuli, by what we speak of as the mind.

Expressions of the Mind

"Generally, there are three categories of mind: the *ordinary mind*, the *transcendental mind* and the *God-Realized Mind*, which is the *Shaman Mind*/Buddha Mind/The Christ Mind/Etc. The first two categories tend to overlap each other and, on occasion, because the essential nature of life is The Void or God Itself, they tend to overlap with the God-Realized Mind, as well. When one establishes the God-Realized Mind as her/his home, however, the influence from the ordinary mind becomes memory-related only, while the supernatural influence of the transcendental mind becomes a natural integration.

"The reason we say that the God-Realized Mind's relationship with the ordinary mind is memory-related only (dead images), is because the fear-based images projected by the ordinary mind interact via what we call mind passions (anger, lust, greed, vanity and attachment and their relationship, impatience, ego, etc.) and these cannot penetrate the living images of the God-Realized Mind.

"The images produced by the ordinary mind correlate to the previous and on-going karmic experiences of the individual; that is, such images reflect one's personality - traits, talents, attitudes, opinions and fears. The ordinary mind is the home of the habitual reactive mind, where the individual is compelled by habits, addictions and obsessions, controlled by fear of success and failure and by all other dualities. However, when the movement of one's consciousness develops into the courage to intercept these limiting behaviors, one begins to transcend these related passions and the individual then begins to enliven an acceptance for personal freedom, which gradually expands one's personal awareness to *realize* that all life experiences result from the source of one's attention, and that the individual alone, rules his/her own life with the essential power of *choice.*

"The *transcendental mind* (transformational mind) encapsulates psychic energy, and in its most refined and evolved state, can act as an image-energizer that expresses the images projected by the *God-Realized Mind* into the world. In this integrated process - the transcendental mind with the God-Realized Mind - expresses the God force into the environment, which then acts as a catalyst to serve, to awaken and to enlighten others.

"Of course, the evolved *transcendental* mind we speak of no longer electrically charges or reflects fearful image pictures that psychically controlled the *ordinary mind.* The horror shows are gone. Instead, the pictures imaged in a person's mind are refined, which also means that the life of the individual is refined. This is because whatever a person images, represents their state of mind, which projects their mental outlook into the environment. Such images then, literally, become the life of the individual. In other words, however one sees life is how their life is lived.

"Before we continue, it is important that we clear up a misunderstanding of this process. We are not evoking visualization or techniques that *conjure* images to mind. These misguided practices, such as visualizing money into your life, tend to glorify fantasy, which the objective mind argues into conflicting images. The conflicting images that are set up in the objective mind through such image conjuring, more often than not, cancel the positive images and replace them with fear, or feelings of being unworthy to receive what is desired. As such, the person who conjures a vision of money can very likely end up in a role of handling someone else's money, such as a bank teller.

"To achieve a desired goal, one must keep their eye on the bulls-eye and proceed as Soul. *As Soul* means to live with your attention at the Third Eye or what I call Soul Vision. As Soul one naturally lives in abundance; that is, whatever one desires is at hand. This is because Soul is part of God, The Void, which is both *nothing* and *all things*. When this state is lived consciously, there exists **only** the *God-Realized Mind*, the Universal or One Mind. The nature of the *One Mind* that we speak of, is expressed as *divine* love. Divine love cannot be conjured via a visualization technique, because it is the resulting condition of one who lives consciously <u>as</u> Soul. As a person evolves to this consciousness, he or she learns that <u>choice</u> can be exercised, to accept something or a condition into their life. The individual then recognizes that the simplicity of choice is a power to remove one from the role of *'being a victim of circumstances'* that indeed, one cannot be a victim as long as he is acting out his life by exercising his rights as an individual to choose what he wants.

"This stage of mind is in continual evolvement, a process of refinement. As an individual progresses on the Path of Soul, more and more, one's mind pictures project images of beauty - from beautiful scenery, to scenes of warmth and compassion for other people, animals and other living things. In other words, a smile on a person's face projects radiance into one who lives from the transcendental mind, which ignites their mind into transformational love, and that projects clarity and joy and freedom into their relationships in life. Thus, one steps into the arena of an illuminated mind, where an even greater process begins to unfold - the never-ending evolvement of an awakening consciousness, the merger of becoming ONE with God.

"May the blessings be."

"The transcendental mind (transformational mind) encapsulates psychic energy, and in its most refined and evolved state, can act as an image-energizer that expresses the images projected by the God-Realized Mind into the world."

Deities

After HŪMing, Easy Walker asked Winged Wolf if she would talk about the meaning of a banner depicting a Tibetan deity that hung in the Happy House.

Winged Wolf: "When I was a child, Mr. X[1] gave me a little tan book about Milarepa, and in the book, there was a picture of the deity, Chenrezigs[2]. I knew the name was Chenrezigs, only I called it something like Fuziwig or Chessiewig.

"Chenrezigs was explained to me as an *idea* of love and compassion presented in symbolic form to teach the nature of divine love. He is depicted as a many armed figure, to define the ability to give compassion to all sentient beings. Of course, Chenrezigs became an idea of love and compassion long before my memories; however, my memories extend a long way back, long ago when I knew Mr. X and others like him in other lifetimes.

"So, Chenrezigs continues to be an idea of love. Now so many people put their attention on Chenrezigs, He has become a powerful living Being; an embodiment of compassion itself. When I say a *living Being*, I mean He personifies a living Being. He lives on Earth through Being alive in Eastern religion. He has become imprinted in the hearts of people as the representative of compassion and divine love. That is how

---

[1] Mr. X was a Spiritual Teacher to Winged Wolf when she was a child, visible only to herself. Mr. X defined his visitations with her as doubling.

[2] Pronounced sPan-ras-gzigs; Tibetan form of Avalokiteshvara, the Buddha with many hands.

Chenrezigs came into being, and this is how most deities are formed.

"If enough people believe in a deity and follow the teachings that specific deity represents, then the deity becomes embodied on the physical plane. IT becomes real by being embodied in the hearts and the minds of people. Chenrezigs is embodied in Eastern homes by statues and he resembles what he personifies, as he appears in the banner hanging behind me. If you really look at his personification, you will see what he is about. Look (pointing to the banner behind her) at his multitude of giving hands. They are open and turned into the heart. In other words, study an image and you will know what IT represents.

"A deity is a private idea and it is a public idea. It is a private idea, made public. It is an exposure of the heart, made public."

Wings of Change: "Is a deity a mental invention?"

"Absolutely, but a mental invention deliberately presented and propagated by Soul. In other words, Soul fashioned an image of compassion in Chenrezigs. Chenrezigs, was/is 'out there' to uplift. If you pray to Chenrezigs, you are saying, 'I give myself in service to humanity and I pledge myself to spread compassion.' So, it is important to know what you put your attention upon."

Easy Walker: "Like icons?"

"Yes, but some icons or images are often out there just to control the people, such as religions.... statues of a man with a bleeding heart or a person being tortured on a cross. Whoever witnesses them is led to feelings of guilt. Jesus Christ was not a deity but a human Being embodying divine love.

Wings of Change: "I just realized that the word 'humanity' starts with the HUM."

"Yes, Humanity starts with the HÜM, (referring to the vibration/sound of the Void) but the HÜM too, is also an icon. It is an icon of the vibration."

Wings of Change: "So, the vibration Is and the HÜM is an icon of It."

"Yes, people can sing the HÜM in different ways, and that is okay."

Silent Feathers: "If I were to think of compassion, I might have a difficult time trying to HÜM it."

"You wouldn't if you had, in front of you, an individual who needed that compassion. This is where it connects. A deity is an icon, a vehicle."

(Looking at Silent Feathers)

"I know you are imaging the many deities you have seen in your travels to Eastern Countries and you are trying to put the pieces together, so please listen carefully. If the deities give people refinement rather than fear, then the deities were invented as a symbol for Soul consciousness. If they propagate fear and guilt feelings, then they come from someone's mind, a mind that says, *'You have got to keep the people under control.'* And, there are many religions that do that.

"How can you be uplifted by looking at someone suffering? To show you the results of your actions so that you walk around saying, *'Father, forgive me, Father, forgive me, Father, forgive me'*, then, all you do is feel ashamed of yourself all the time. If you are feeling ashamed of yourself, how can you live as Soul? Soul is not ashamed. Soul is an embodiment of divine love. Parents propagate shame in their children, because shame was pushed into them - Shame, Shame, Shame, Shame. People use shame on their offspring so that the children will not do certain things; but actually, there is no value to shame at all.

"Deities play an important role in our lives, and you can see how they stand out in our society."

Easy Walker: "Yes, but they are make-believe."

"Well, they are make-believe, but when they are make-believe to so many people, they are also real. What do you think the environment is? One person mentally invents this place and another person adds to it. As soon as you look at it, you add to it, then somebody else looks at it, and adds to it. You see, the environment is nothing more than an accumulation of energy. Deities are nothing more than accumulated energy. Chenrezigs is a great, powerful ball of energy and the culture that He came from is also a powerful ball of energy. People are also products of their culture."

Easy Walker: "So these pictures become a reminder of what the images represent."

"Yes, and Milarepa (a Tibetan 11th Century Saint), is a symbol of power in a gentle form, one who could totally overcome the worst of karma. If he could do it, you and I could do it. Do you see?

"So, what are you an embodiment of? Well, you do not know yet, but you are getting there. Each person is an embodiment of their energy. Chenrezigs may not have a physical body, but in a way he does, because there are many images of him, so he is personified. You have a physical body that is composed of your karma. In a way you are similar, do you see?"

(All apprentices break into gales of laughter as Winged Wolf pinches her cheek in different places for about 20 seconds).

"As I pinch my face, it is really my karma you are looking at. This is how I have taken care of myself. It is what I came back with in this life; who I evolved into being at this point. *You are looking at my karma. I am looking at your karma.*"

Easy Walker: That makes perfect sense to me, perfect sense. Thank you."

"So, to say my body is mentally invented, is true. It is an embodiment of my karma. It was invented by my mentality, as I evolved. Now, next lifetime, if I were to come back, it will be more evolved yet. The environment, you see, is an evolvement of karma and the way you look at it, and the way you put your energy into it and the way the next person puts their energy on it. It keeps changing and evolving. Like the human body, it is an evolvement of karma."

Wings of Change: "When we reincarnate, how will we look?"

"You will look very similar. You will find you would look very similar in this incarnation to what you looked like previously. Your body is an accumulation and evolvement of your karma. So, you look like this now, and next time you will look the same, only a little bit more or less refined, although your body may be another gender."

Easy Walker: "We only know you as Winged Wolf in this life. Will we tap into our connection with you in past lives?"

"You will remember. There will come a point where you will remember who you were, and who I was."

Easy Walker: "Do you know who you were?"

"Yes. And, you will know it too. It is like holding something underwater. The weights are on it, holding it down. The old ropes holding the weights begin to fray as you are exposing your myth, your mental baggage, seeing bits and pieces of who you are <u>not</u>. And, as you begin to live as Soul, what was buried underwater so to speak, begins to surface, to come to the top of the water."

Easy Walker: "And we will be able to look at other people and possibly see who they were?"

"Of course. I am no different from you. You know, I am just an accumulation of my karma too, just as you are."

(There is another big burst of laughter as Winged Wolf starts pinching her cheeks and face again).

Silent Feathers: "So, no matter where each of us is in the present moment, in that present moment, we will always know each other?"

"When that present moment opens itself, yes. I have met the moments in my past and I am still meeting some of those moments. It is in the process of unfolding. But, I have recognized much of my past, which is why I am sitting where I am sitting right now, do you see? And you will come into that understanding of your own accord, not only of myself, but of yourself when you surface.

"I have my head above water. And you are coming up. You are getting closer. That is why you must never push, rush or compete. What in the world would be the point? Everything I do with you, is to help you surface. And, each person I treat differently. What I do with one, I may not do with another, because your karma is individual.

"Maybe the first time I opened a book in my adult years and looked at a picture of Chenrezigs, I did not know why I was so fascinated. I did not exactly remember, but I remembered. Because I was so encased at that point by my own attitudes and opinions about things, I could not remember certain things, but there was some kind of knowing, some kind of surfacing, like the elephant that always surfaced in my subconscious. I always envisioned an elephant nearby.

"You know, I was so crazy about elephants that when I worked in public relations and promoted the grand-opening of a shopping center, I marched an elephant up the street. I had this thing about elephants. *'You gotta have elephants!'* So, I had an elephant walking down the street to the new shopping center to get people's attention. People said, *'Why does she have an elephant?'* I said, *'I don't know, I had to have an elephant.'* I had to parade an elephant. It never occurred to me what my obsession was about. I closed my eyes at night and I would see elephants.

"So, there are these little subtle images you cannot be aware of until they surface. When they surface, the pieces start falling together fast and furiously. It is like, *'Whoa, is that what this has been all about? I have been blind all these years, literally blinded by attitudes and opinions, blocking the real meaning of things.'* The attitudes and opinions acquired form rigid boxes made of, *'Things have to be a certain way!'* They do not.

"My teacher Alana said, *'If I dumped a can of red paint on you, you would get mad at me?'* And I answered, *'Yes I would'.* Then she said, *'Why?',* and I said, *'Well, wouldn't you get mad at me if I dumped a can of red paint on you?'* She then said, *'No, I would think, 'Well, I will just be red today. A bit extreme.'* (Laughter)

"Allow your true self to surface from your attitudes and opinions. Come up to find out who you really are." (Looking at SkyWolf who is deaf). You will realize why your hearing shut down when you can surface enough to see it. Who knows, already you speak about the vibrations alive in your head. The first steps to hearing are those vibrations. Limitations exist only beneath the surface. There are no limitations on the Path of Soul.

"So, when you study something from your myth and you say, *'Well, that can't happen because of this',* remember, you are beneath the surface. Let go of that idea, that little box that says, *'It can't happen that way because...'* let go of it and just don't think about it. It will help you surface a little bit more and, when you get up here, then you can just Be. But, you never have to give up being human. You have earned this body and it functions as properly as you take care of it.

"People think certain things about their bodies are dirty and it is not true. Bodily functions are wonderful. Put something inside and it passes through the system to come out again. And, that is the way life is - You put something into life and it comes back! It is all the same principle."

Wings of Change: "It is pretty simple when you put it that way."

"Life itself is an illusion and yet it is real, because we have invented it here. The body is an illusion, but it is real because it is our karma, hardened into a mass. It is useful as a vehicle for Soul. So, next time you look into the mirror say, *'Oh, I did this!'* (Again, much laughter).

Easy Walker: "I don't have to look!"

"That's right. As you are surfacing, your face is going to change and there are drastic changes in your body. Sometimes you look in the mirror and you may not recognize yourself. *'Oh, who is that?'* Or, you see a photograph, *'Oh, I don't know that person'.*"

Wings of Change: "So you are watching yourself evolve as you let go."

"Yes. It is shocking sometimes, looking at a strange face. One's face is evolving, taking on the characteristics of what you are becoming."

Wings of Change: "Your attitude about suffering is different from my understanding of what Buddha/Christ Consciousness is. They seem to be more enmeshed in the idea that we really had to understand something about suffering to evolve."

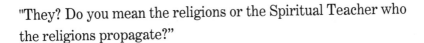

"They? Do you mean the religions or the Spiritual Teacher who the religions propagate?"

Easy Walker: "Well, what about Milarepa? He suffered."

"Yes, but Milarepa suffered because of what he did, the terrible deeds of his past. Gradually, he moved beyond suffering, but it took years of self-discipline to conquer his little self. He had calluses on his buttocks like a horses hooves, from sitting so long in meditation, resolving his karma."

Easy Walker: "It is interesting, as I reflect, that he resisted taking on students, as you initially resisted taking on students."

"It is the result of the evolution of one's consciousness.
    "May the blessings be."

"You will find you would look very similar in this incarnation to what you looked like previously."

Mind vs. Consciousness

Winged Wolf: "Mind and consciousness work together, but the mind is a separate entity. It is a fantasy machine. When one side of the brain interacts with the other side of the brain; that is, the circuitry of the left and right sides of the brain (so popularly talked about today), the mind comes into play. The mind produces images and feelings about the images, creating a fantasy. So that is how a fantasy comes about.

"Consciousness, on the other hand, enlivens an awareness of fantasy, and at the same time, it interacts with the fantasy. When you are living from the Shaman Consciousness, you can deliberately produce fantasies and then you interact with them to present the dream you decide to live and work in.

"You actually take the circuitry of the right side of the brain and you overlap it in a certain way with the left side of the brain to bring about the fantasy you would like to present into the world. And, when we say fantasy, we are really talking about dream images. The images that are produced, are produced in accordance with the state of a person's consciousness. So the mentality or the mind of a person is activated to present images, in accordance with the consciousness of the individual."

Two Eagles: "Is fantasy an image of what we normally call reality, in the physical body and the surroundings we are in?"

"Yes, and it is a reflection of the individual's state of consciousness at the same time. So, while the body and the environment in which it lives are the fantasy, the fantasy is also

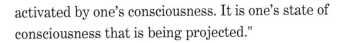

activated by one's consciousness. It is one's state of consciousness that is being projected."

Two Eagles: "That reality is different from God Conscious reality, is that correct?"

"There are three realities: The Void (God) *Is*, Soul *Is*, and Life *Is*; life being the dream of the Void or Soul. The dream comes about from one's mind. The mind is the producer of the dream, which is enacted either consciously or unconsciously. In the case of a person who is unconscious that life is a dream, unconscious images bring about the cause of worry, fear, and despair. From these, the person gets himself into greater trouble by magnifying what he is worried about. His attitudes magnify what he has attitudes about, and his opinions magnify what he has opinions about. But this is all unconscious.

"With the conscious person, or the person living as Soul from the Shaman Consciousness, all life is deliberate. Such a Consciousness dictates what will be and also interacts with what is going on. But as the conscious person presents life, he or she does not manipulate other people or situations; instead the person realizes that what exists is a projection of their state of being, a consciousness of it. In other words, one's consciousness has awareness, or it can lack awareness, depending upon one's degree of awakening.

"Where is the attention? Wherever the attention is, that is where the awareness is and the consciousness expands on that."

Two Eagles: "So the level of consciousness determines the level of mind being used?"

"A conscious person, one who is living as Soul, is very selective where the attention is placed because that is what expands."

Two Eagles: "The mind places the attention, is that correct, is that the vehicle for placing attention?"

"It is a matter of which came first, the chicken or the egg, because somewhere along the line, attitudes were formed through images that the brain saw or conjured up through the mind's experience, which made the brain's electrical circuitry cross in a certain place to produce that image. Attitudes can be formed through watching a TV show, or hearing about somebody else's experience in life, a facsimile, that would bring about the image.

"Understanding this may slip in and then slip away; it slips in and it slips away. It does this because we are talking about something that is very elusive. It does not exist in ordinary language. We are talking about the fantasy."

Two Eagles: "The mind is a fantasy?"

"The mind itself is a fantasy, yes, because it exists as a result of interactions between the left brain and the right brain. *The mind is both the fantasy machine and the fantasy itself.* The capacity of interaction of the two brains is the fantasy machine, resulting from electrical circuits from the left brain to the right brain going 'buzzzzzit' and it's the 'buzzzzzit' that is the mind imaging. (Laughter) So, wherever the attention rests, is what causes the overlapping from one side of the brain to the other and it goes 'buzzzzzit', do you see?"

Two Eagles: "Uh huh...Can a person function without the mind?"

"You always have to use this 'buzzzzit' mind. If you don't, you have no life to live. The mind projects images of the environment so that we can live in it. So we may be making fun of it by saying it's the buzzzzzit of the electrical circuitry, but at the same time, the mind is a vital part of our existence. It is what creates the images we live. It is what produces the environment we walk through. As Soul, we deliberately choose images that are uplifting and happy, focusing on mind-pleasing scenes. When the mind produces scenes that are pleasing to it, it does not make horror shows; it does not make life unpleasant. So, when people are studying the left brain versus the right brain, it is not correct to divide the brain, by saying, *'I'm a right brain person versus a left brain person',* because both sides always work together. You might be predominantly creative or very imaginative because of the nature of the type of person you are, left or right handed. Imaginative means that one side of the brain may be more dominant when it short circuits the other side of the brain and goes *bussssz* rather than *buzzzzit,* do you see? (Laughter) We're really reducing it here, but it is a fact.

"So, the images that come to the brain may go *'lahhhhha'* when they are a little flowery, or when they are not as flowery, they may be horror shows; or they are brilliant ideas, or they are ordinary ideas."

"From the Shaman Consciousness, you work from the balanced part of your brain. You keep your mind and your brain moving in deliberate action; you are at the balance point when you consciously produce your images. You are at the balance point but sometimes, in order to get a mind-pleasing scene out of something, you definitely might go over to the other side. Do you see? But it is all deliberate. The Shaman Consciousness always

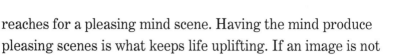

reaches for a pleasing mind scene. Having the mind produce pleasing scenes is what keeps life uplifting. If an image is not pleasing, do not look at it.

"So, the Shaman Consciousness knows how to use the circuitry in the brain to produce the pleasing scenes for the mind, then the pleasing scenes are perpetuated rather than the horror show being perpetuated. It perpetuates itself as a beautiful scene. Then that beautiful scene is given to the person who meets the individual and that individual gives the pleasing images to another person, and so on. It's like handing someone a bouquet of flowers and they hand the bouquet of flowers to someone else."

Two Eagles: "Where does attention originate or come from?"

"Attention originates from your senses, from where you place your eyes, from what you listen to. Yesterday, I asked you to listen to the space between sounds. In that silence between sounds, you are in the Shaman Consciousness. In that space between the sights, you are in the Shaman Consciousness. In that space between feelings, you are in the Shaman Consciousness. But the easiest way to grasp the meaning of this, is through listening. Listen between the sounds. Listening will put you in a state of constant diligence."

Two Eagles: "It is quite interesting."

"The result is total quiet within one's brain, but in that total quiet, the brain is ready to be activated at any second. So there is motion in the stillness."

Two Eagles: "I am realizing I normally listen for sound and this is a different cadence than to listen to sounds."

"Listen <u>to</u> the silence between the sounds."

Two Eagles: "It seems to be a shift."

"It really is a shift."

Two Eagles: "I also hear many things I would not normally hear by doing that. I hear birds flying in the distance, wings beating..."

"So it expands the awareness."

Two Eagles: "Absolutely!"

Trailblazer: "That's when the whole body essentially becomes an organ too, doesn't it?"

"Yes, it does. Your entire body is a sensory organ. Now this body that is a sensory organ was manifested out of all of your mind stuff, past and present (karma). That is why you see it changing so much, because it is becoming refined."

Trailblazer: "Is that why you look so different too, or is that my perception?"

"Well, it is always both, which is the same thing. As a person moves along the Path; there is no end to the Path, so naturally, the person is constantly looking different, and they can have a thousand faces... or more... or less." (Laughter)

Two Eagles: "So, once conscious, you can dream any dream you wish."

"That is correct. You can dream any dream you want, if you have an anchor to hold you to look in a particular direction."

Two Eagles: "So, your apprentices are an anchor?"

"Yes, along with my desire to go as far as I can go in this lifetime. Now, when I have apprentices who are peers, there will be a real beginning point. When I say peers, they may not be necessarily where I stand, but they are on a consciousness level where they are beginning, because the Shaman Consciousness is the real *beginning*. It is the real beginning.... beginning.... beginning.... beginning.... beginning. When someone comes to the point of that beginning, then the anchor will be elaborated. And there will be much more freedom."

Two Eagles: "We are just getting ready to start!"

"Yes."

Two Eagles: "Well, it felt like, in listening to the silence, I had to reverse myself because it was totally opposite of how I would normally be."

"Yes, you are always listening to sounds. In this way you are listening to the silence between the sounds, which is a wonderful exercise for anyone on the spiritual path.
"May the blessings be."

"Yesterday J asked you to listen to the space between sounds. Jn that silence between sounds, you are in the Shaman Consciousness."

Textures of Karma

Winged Wolf: "I heard one of you say, *'yesterday was a doozy'*. You learned many things yesterday; we experienced many things together, and through our experiences together, you saw many things about yourselves, and what you saw about yourself was your karmic *textures.*

"You *felt* the textures you had become, through your actions and your reactions to things, or the karma that you have developed. Texture comes about in your life as you set a button in your consciousness that says, *'I am this way or I am that way.'* Out of that, there gets to be a little *feel* to you that other people sense when they come in contact with you. Others respond to you by the feeling that you put out there. That feeling is the texture, or the weave of your own cloth, the weave of your personality and your karma.

"Yesterday, I pointed out what that texture looks like. I responded to you, or did not respond to you, according to what you were putting out and what you needed to learn. I put each of you on the pond, on a raft or in a boat and after a time, I asked each of you a question: *'What have you experienced from being on the water?'*

"One answer that came back was about the ripples on the surface of the water; how every movement was seen as a ripple that spiraled outward. Another person told me about the mirror effect on the surface of the pond and how she saw her consciousness reflected, like in a dream world.

"Another person gave me answers that were not quite on target, because she was saying things she felt I wanted to hear. And each time I went back and asked her the same question, I got a different answer. This individual was the last one off the pond; night was falling and it was getting cold. After she repeatedly tried to give me an acceptable answer, I decided to send my jacket out to her. But in the process, one more time, I asked, *'Tell me the texture, the true texture of what you are learning.'* And she turned to me and said, *'I am learning that you do not want me to answer just to please you. You want me to answer from my heart.'* At which point she was free to leave the pond. She came in and got warm.

"The textures you set up in life are textures and ideas from other people, from society, from newspapers, from television, from schools, from parents, from friends, who have also been infiltrated and textured with all of those associations. You say to yourself, *'This is what I am to be like. So when I am with these people, I behave in this way.'* But, when you come here, you are not sure how to behave. After awhile you learn that you are to behave impeccably to your own nature and that is all I want from you. That is the texture of your true cloth, that true cloth of Soul who knows Itself.

"When you know yourself, then you are able to look at the textures of all things and identify them, their makeup, how they were put together and why they were put together. All the energy of that texture tells you those many things, just by looking at it. You can see what the web was like as the weaving was done. And you can see many of the weaver's influences.

"So there is a texture of personality and there is a texture of impeccability, which is whatever the moment calls forth. It is not a rigid design in the piece of cloth. It is your own expression of the Void, not someone else's expression. Although you can have a similar expression as someone else, there is a genuineness that comes through in the expression, while it is coming through you as the expresser. If you are merely being a puppet, reciting what somebody else says, then that person who is living as Soul looking at you, can feel the influence of where you are coming from and what you are trying to project. As Soul, it is easy to see when you are playing the role of a pretender. When you put down the pretender role and you become genuinely yourself, then your impeccability, your connection to the Void, is expressed purely and divinely.

'I have come to realize that you do not want me to say as everybody else says; you want me to speak for myself.'

"Yes!

"Life has many textures to it and it contains textures from everyone who lives within it. Life also contains facsimile textures. It contains original textures of yourself expressing the Void, expressing divine or unconditional love through your actions. Life also contains other textures, aberrated textures of one doing things to please other people to win approval by copying other people's ways, because their way looks as if it might be better than what you know as right, because you doubt yourself.

"There is also the texture of very fine impeccability, whereby you take what you know to be true and you magnify it into the world. This has a texture that is smooth, or coarse sometimes, coarse in a magnificent way. And that is the way of The Spiritual Teacher. The Spiritual Teacher sometimes is coarse in a magnificent way, magnificent because she or he uplifts another person, rather than puts him down. *Smooth* because it is easy to be smooth, in *service.* Impeccability is the texture of service.

"It is the texture of one's capability and one's easability to love. (pause) And it is the texture of impeccability in that loving.

Whatever is needed to be said to uplift is said, even though it may feel coarse and rough for a moment. It is the magnificent coarseness that makes it smooth. It's like rubbing a piece of sandpaper over a rough piece of wood. Does that tell you about texture?"

Easy Walker: "That puts a new meaning to the word 'coarse' and 'texture', by saying the teacher is coarse and magnificent to uplift.... Coarse means rough to me and I have difficulty seeing how you use the word 'coarse'..."

"Can you say that a piece of sandpaper is not magnificent? Yet it is coarse when it meets the wood and it rubs upon it to make it smooth."

Easy Walker: "It does...it does, so, yes...."

"And then when the wood is smoother, The Teacher uses a finer piece of sandpaper, extra-fine."

Easy Walker: "So I guess when you grab our handles (myth), that is possibly the coarseness you work with..."

"It feels coarse to you."

Easy Walker: "It really does, I never thought of it that way, but..."

"It feels a little coarse to me too. Sometimes it's like 'Oh!' You know, but I have to do it."

Easy Walker: "It brings clarity to it."

"That's right. It's a magnificent coarseness, you see?"

Easy Walker: "Oh thank you, yeah, it is."

"It's not a coarseness that makes you feel like you have to grovel or you stay miserable if the coarseness rubs over you."

Easy Walker: "I guess my impeccability in my dream was when you told me to look at my texture; it must have been how my texture changed being with other people, and as a result I changed. So, my impeccability, as I see it, is to be true to myself."

"That's right. And the truth is getting to find out who you are, yourself, and not the facsimile image of who you think you are. And you are getting close to that."

Easy Walker: "When Jackson (dog) woke me up scratching at the door, I woke up (from the dream)with your telling me to 'Be aware of your texture.' and I thought, 'I've got to write this one down,' it was so clear. Thank you."

"You're welcome."

Wolfsong: "I was thinking about the reflection in the pond as a facsimile to what is above the water and a facsimile of ourselves of what we're putting out there, or think we should be, or whatever, is that what you're saying about facsimiles....I'm trailing around here?"

"What is your question?"

Wolfsong: "Well, you asked me yesterday about what the reflection in the pond was and I felt it didn't have substance that it was the reflection and..."

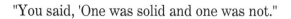

"You said, 'One was solid and one was not."

Wolfsong: "Right."

"How are you any more solid? How is your body any more solid than the water that it was reflected upon? Your body is a composite of your karma, nothing more. It was your karma reflected on a mass; the mass is also your karma. Your mass of karma then was reflected on the water, which is also a mass.

"You did not realize what you were saying. I asked you to tell me what you had learned and you went off on a fantasy. You told me what you had supposed, not what you had learned. You are not the water and you are not your body, yet you are your body and you are the water.

"If you see yourself in the water, you are the water. If you see yourself in the sky, you are the sky. If you see yourself in me, you are me. If you see yourself in a movie, you are the movie, the character(s) in the movie. What attracts you, you identify with. What you identify with, you become.

"When you have an attraction to a movie, it is because you are seeing yourself and, narcissistically, you have a companion who is like you. If that companion breaks out of the mold, then you feel you are breaking out of the mold. But that is not necessarily so, is it? The mere fact that the character in the movie breaks out of the mold does not mean that you have broken out of the mold. Because your reflection in the pond looks a certain way, it does not mean that you look that certain way. Because you have taken on the texture of water, does not mean that the mass body that you carry has taken on the texture of water, even though it is composed mostly of water.

"In contrast, one day you will see that all life is ONE, not just in an intellectual sense, but you will recognize yourself as a part of all life."

Wolfsong: "And in what way can any of us know that?"

"Texture - the habitual ways of thinking have formed your texture or the karma that you carry around as a body and your mind.... a body, a brain, that forms your mind. The body, the brain, forms pictures that are projected upon what we call the mind. Mind projects these like a motion picture. It is the video camera pumping out the images of electrical currents as they flash across. We see them with our physical eyes as the environment in which we live. They come from the texture, your karma. When those images become refined enough, then you will be able to see it. Then you will consciously become omnipresent. Then you will *play* in a way, which you don't know about now.
"May the blessings be."

" *Life has many textures to it and it contains textures from everyone who lives within it.*"

Visions and the Natural State

Winged Wolf: "The consciousness of an individual makes the vision that produces an image. The image then, is really the lower aspect of the mind; the vision is what comes up just above it; and the consciousness is what propels the whole thing into motion.

"Science can make a body; it can now clone a sheep. When using DNA to clone a body, a karmic duplication is effected out of organic material. Now, if you were to use inorganic material or matter that did not contain DNA, there could be no karmic duplication, which means there could not be a consciousness attached to it, because consciousness and karma live together. In other words, when karma attaches, the consciousness springs forth. You see, karma cannot exist without consciousness, nor can consciousness exist in a physical body without karma, or it could exist only briefly, as in the flick of a switch, but even then, the flick of the switch would have been from some minuscule bit of karma.

"To sustain life, consciousness *has* to be attached to a body. Or in other words, life can be sustained as long as there is karmic activity in propulsion. If karmic activity is in propulsion, then there is a consciousness attached to it.

"..... Visions and the *Natural State*. When you see something, you are imaging it, which is a vision. Vision comes from the nature of the consciousness that you are operating from, which is stimulated by your awareness to produce karma in consciousness. Consciousness is like the hub of the wheel that

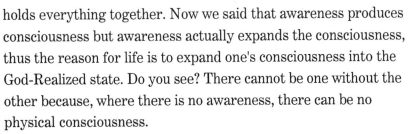

holds everything together. Now we said that awareness produces consciousness but awareness actually expands the consciousness, thus the reason for life is to expand one's consciousness into the God-Realized state. Do you see? There cannot be one without the other because, where there is no awareness, there can be no physical consciousness.

"When we speak of one's awareness and one's consciousness as separate entities, we do so only to see how one's awareness of something can produce a consciousness of it, although on the physical plane, awareness and consciousness are not really separate. Nothing we have ever talked about is separate or different in subject matter, because all aspects of life are really the same. And yet, if you were to mentally throw out a postulation of, *'This is the same as this',* I would say, *'No, it is not',* because you see, that would be your viewpoint of how you are looking at it, rather than seeing the subject(s) as a whole."

Winged Wolf turns to apprentice Wide Eyes,

"Yesterday I asked you to circumambulate around the Happy House one hundred times; then later, after an hour or so, I asked you, *'How many laps have you done?* And, you said, *'I don't know, I didn't count. It doesn't matter.'* And I said that it did matter, because I had asked you to do something.... (There is a short moment of quiet, and Winged Wolf lovingly says,) And then, finally, you got the message and began counting your hundred laps. You look very good after all that exercise. (Meaning Wide Eyes had walked a total of more than 4 miles.)

"What you learned was that your attitude, *'It's all the same, nothing matters,'* bunches things together to form a fantasy about a point of view that isolated you from the request.

"Operating from a set attitude always presents a limited point of view, so much so that one automatically makes the postulation of, *'Oh well, it doesn't matter',* and it does matter. You see (again looking at Wide Eyes), I gave you instructions to do something a certain way to show you how you act about things. I wanted you to see yourself. You took a little ball of wax, acceptance in yourself of, *'Oh well, I don't care what she does to me. I am just going to go ahead and do this,'* while you are saying you didn't care, you brushed my request aside. So, you were really walking around the Happy House your way, from *your* point of view of the teachings I have written about. (Winged Wolf is referring to a teaching that she wrote about in *Woman Between the Wind* referred to as the three rules of life - 1) It doesn't matter; 2) You don't need to understand everything, and 3) There is no competition.)

"A person sometimes tries to rationalize a reaction in an effort to pacify their resignation in this way. Such responses to spiritual principles are something a spiritual teacher has to help a person work through, especially when that person is a dedicated student on the Path of Soul who feels she is acting out what the teacher wants. She was really living a teaching out of context, and not really doing what was requested of her. (Winged Wolf slowly looks at each apprentice.) There is a fine line here.

"You see, we are talking about one's visions of things and the natural state. The *natural state* is a place of power that each person has to prepare to enter. When I say, *'prepare',* I mean that one has to remove *their preconceived ideas* about what he thinks exists, so that he can be aware of what actually does exist. If the commander of a ship were to hold fast to a procedure that he learned at the Naval Academy, in lieu of an assessment of the true state of a situation, he may get his ship in trouble. In difficult straits, a good commander will often place himself in his captain's shoes in order to see a critical situation through his captain's eyes. He tries to enter the state of awareness that his captain commands from, to handle the critical situation accordingly.

"You know, if the captain is off the ship in trouble somewhere and his commander is in charge, the commander is required to respond like the captain. In a critical situation, he steps into the captain's shoes, and it could mean the captain's death, because he is living out the situation through the captain's eyes, which is the way he has been trained to carry out his duty. Now, you may never have to lose a captain in your life. This is not what we are really talking about. We are saying that situations are clear through a true spiritual teacher's eyes, which shows the action that needs to be taken. In other words, within the shadows or difficult moments of life, there always exists the *natural state*. The vision that occurs to one who lives in the *natural state* comes from the God Consciousness, and it is uncluttered and unfettered by fantasy or myth. From the *natural state*, one sees *exactly* what energy is being portrayed, which is why in a difficult time you would ask yourself, *'What would my spiritual teacher do?'* You might even silently call upon her or him for help - a prayer for help.

"Without experience, one may have difficulty trusting their own vision, and this means that, if someone wandered into the *natural state* and, for a brief instant, saw something, he would, most likely, doubt what he saw. You know, he is not accustomed to such a clear vision of existence; he is not accustomed to seeing beyond illusion, beyond the dual worlds. He might be awed into having the realization of such a moment cling to him for a very long time. Realization from God Consciousness can be a shock and it is the shock that clings to him, not the experience of viewing the *Natural State* itself. Such an individual can remain in shock for a very short time or a very long time, depending upon their karmic balance.

"When a person is accustomed to living in the *natural state*, the visions perceived are not upsetting to behold. While the *natural state* is ever-clarifying, evolving and therefore new to experience, one becomes accustomed to Its uniqueness and becomes comfortable in It. The *natural state* doesn't lose Its beauty or clarity or become ordinary, ever. One simply becomes more accustomed to the energy that evolves Its clarity and beauty, to look into the *natural state* is to see an aliveness that is uncluttered with fantasy, even though the subject being viewed is illusionary. One can see how fantasy or illusion lives in the individual who invented it. In other words, the consciousness from where an individual views life, duplicates the energy of the fantasies from where that person lives.

"Fantasies are often built from *mind poisons*, which are what we call the emotions of life. Emotions are such feelings born from vanity (ego), anger (frustration, impatience), lust (obsession urges), greed (dissatisfied or discontentment), and attachment (possessiveness). These are the 'little self' poisons, birthed by fear. When one lives in the *natural state*, there is no fear. There is divine, unconditional love and compassion; and these two expressions give rise to freedom and joy, which is a state of living as Soul or living in service within your chosen work/life field.

"The true vision of life reflects the purity of the *natural state* Itself....

The *natural state* being the Void.

The *natural state* being God.

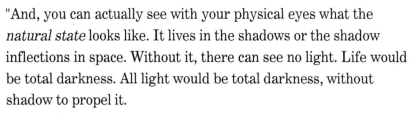
"And, you can actually see with your physical eyes what the *natural state* looks like. It lives in the shadows or the shadow inflections in space. Without it, there can see no light. Life would be total darkness. All light would be total darkness, without shadow to propel it.

"You can hear the Void. You can listen to It as a high-pitched sensation, or you can listen to It in sounds as they are replicated within the environment....birds, rivers, wind in the trees, etc. Through your awareness of sound, you can identify yourself as being one with the *natural state* and live between sound.

"Learn to sit in the silence. I do not use the term meditation for many reasons. In most people's minds, meditation denotes holding thoughts and images from you, and few people are really successful at doing this. What usually happens is, as soon as you step out of meditation, there is usually a burst of distractions, and then you think you have failed. When sitting in the silence, you hold nothing back. You allow thoughts and images to flow through your consciousness. You use those moments when images flow to enliven yourself within the silence, by tuning into the pockets of stillness between the images and the silence between the mind chatter. In so doing, you will gain gradual control of your mind to the point where you can live within the *natural state* while living in propelled motion, actively participating in life.

"Higher consciousness means to be spiritually *awake!* If you are conscious <u>only</u> of your body, then you are not awake, because your body is dominating your consciousness; whereas, when you live as Soul, you can go ahead and note discomfort in your body and still be 100% with the moment, which translates to mean living within the *natural state.*

"A vision of life that occurs within the *natural state* is a reflection of the clarity of your own mind, as it presents pictures for you to view; therefore, the pictures are *always* what you want. They are always beautiful. If there is no vision, there is no life.

"May the blessings be."

"*When we speak of one's awareness and one's consciousness as separate entities, we do so only to see how one's awareness of something can produce a consciousness of it.*"

Divination

Winged Wolf: "I want to talk about the common threads of divination and divination systems - from astrology to numerology, to the I Ching, to the MO and Runes, to reading cards of any kind, to dousing for oil and water, and so on. You may be thinking, my goodness, we are going to be here forever, except that, and this is a very important fact.... All divination systems basically work from the same principles.

"When I was a child my brother and I discovered a magical use for the Bible, that now may sound a little peculiar, but what we did was, we placed a pair of scissors in the center of the Bible, point down, and then we strapped the Bible together with a belt, the two scissor handles sticking out. The belt had to be pulled real tight so that the scissors did not slip out. Then, one of us sat on one side, and the other sat on the opposite side, and each of us balanced a side of the scissor's handle on the very tip of our index fingers. When we were ready, one of us asked a question, while, the other read a passage that we had copied from the Bible, and the passage was from Ruth, *'Whither thou goest I will go,'* that phrase.

"So, my brother would ask, *'Am I going to get an A on my algebra test?'* And if the answer was *'yes'* this Bible would turn, and if the answer was 'no' it would stay still. So we answered many of our teenage questions this way, and then later on, you know, we learned about pendulums, which follows the same principles of operation.

"The energy that gives the answer is really our own energy. In using a pendulum, our energy is released through our fingertips to display for us what we inwardly sense to be true, or what we would like to do, bypassing our fear-related mental conflict that says, *'I may not get what I want.'* If the pendulum turns or spirals, the answer indicated is *'yes.'* If it does not move, it means *'no.'* The answers obtained, however, do not necessarily indicate the wisest action to take, but they do tell us our feelings in the matter.

"Human beings are often attached to the idea that there is greater power dictating their fate, and in ordinary consciousness this is true, because from the ordinary consciousness one is victimized by their lack of conscious awareness. Once an individual is willing to accept responsibility for himself, his choices and actions, or lack of action, he no longer blames or praises a dictating power for his circumstances, or claims that a divine power exists outside of Soul, the individual comes to realize himself as Soul and comes to realize his identification with God the Void. At the moment that *realization* clicks into place, the power of the God-Force is no longer manifest outside the individual, but instead resides within the individual consciousness.

"But getting back to divination systems, there are many methods -Tarot Cards, Medicine Cards, Angel Cards, the MO Dice, Rune Tiles, etc. When using them, it is vital to remember that, the cards fall a certain way, or the dice fall a certain way, because of the attraction and repulsion that is existent in the individual's personal nature at the moment he is using the system. This attraction and repulsion is formed out of the person's karmic identity. In other words, each of us attracts certain circumstances relative to our karma, and the divination system extracts messages from that. Once again, like attracts like. When an apprentice draws a topic from the large crystal bowl we have here in the Happy House that is full of questions for discussion, the question that is drawn is attached to the one who draws it. So, when I ask you to pick a topic from the bowl (without looking at the questions), I knew that you would intuitively pick a subject that would be important for you to hear, and that is why I ask you to do that. Consider this: Divination itself may not seem important to you, but the energy that is enlivened within divination is very important to you. Much is known about you by what you choose. In other words, your choices are a form of divination.

"When people play with Ouija boards, sometimes they draw in astral entities. The energy of an astral entity can actually merge with their bodies to speak through them. Bear in mind, however, an astral entity is a disembodied energy whose consciousness is composed and limited by its memory of a previous life and has no perception of present life or present life choices. It attaches to a living being through *like* or similar memory experiences that are fiber-like. If you have ever walked head-on into a thick cobweb, you know the feeling of this kind of attachment. Such feelings aside, however, I do not advise these types of communication, because the dead images of an astral being have a way of clinging to one with a body in order to have physical expression. For instance, if you smoke cigarettes or drink alcohol, an astral entity may be attracted to you to satisfy its craving, which it can no longer satisfy itself. All of the mind passions invite astral attachment.

"Deceased loved ones will often visit you in your sleep dreams for awhile after their translation (death) before they gradually they move on to linger in a memory-related fantasy until, when a karmic attraction draws them back into physical life again. Sometimes, this process is quick and it is sometimes very, very slow, spanning hundreds of physical years.

"Whatever the case, I do not advise using the Ouija board to contact your deceased loved ones, because often another discarnate being will respond instead of the one you love. Just because someone is dead does not mean that he or she will tell you the truth, unless, of course, he was truthful in life. It is, therefore, best to simply let go and allow the process of translation to take place. After a time, your loved one will be reborn and, if there is a family member about to give birth, the loved one will very likely make use of that birth canal to return to life again. Deceased domestic animals cling to human family units in this same way. Even though I have had many different types of dogs and cats in my life, I contend that I have had only one dog and one cat. The traits of one animal inhabit the next one that comes into my life. It amazes me that, while each dog or cat is individual, there are certain characteristics passed on, one to the other.

"So, the Ouija board (or channeling experience) basically tells you your own feelings through connections with a disembodied entity, via your memory related feelings that connect onto the projection of that entity. If you do not have a mental state that connects to the attracted entity, that entity could not relate to you, you see. It is the connection, the mental state that prompts the connection to make it possible for an entity to enter your body.

"Now, sometimes a person who is alive will enter your body, as well. For instance, I have a paralyzed mother and, on occasion, I miss my visiting day with her because of my busy schedule. A night or two later, following the day I was supposed to visit with her, while I am asleep, she will enter my body.

When this happens, I always awaken with a start, because I can feel her paralysis in my body. For a few moments, I cannot move, until in the silence, I accept her feeling of loneliness to see me, and then the experience fades. Of course, wisdom says the next day I must go to visit her.

"Such intimate communication means that the connection between us is very strong; a parent-child connection is the strongest of all physical connections. We are bound by a string of energy that cannot be broken except through death.

"If you become involved with a fortune-teller, such as a card reader, crystal ball gazer, tea leaf reader, etc., you are being imprinted by the mental and karmic intricacies of that person's psyche, interconnecting to their mental states to enable them to interpret you psychically. It is a *given* that the fortune-teller is not living as Soul, because no one who consciously lives as Soul would fortune-tell.

"Warning: A fortune-teller, because he/she does not live as Soul, unconsciously projects their personality traits, their fears, their attitudes and their opinions into such a reading.

"Therefore, they may tell you, *'Oh, you know, you're going to have a big change in your life,'* because the fortune-teller fears or senses, or knows about a change in his life, which then complicates your life by him telling you your fortune in a related way. Now, as you are going about your day, you say to yourself, *'Well I don't want to do this because I'm going to have a big change in my life,'* see? So you begin to direct yourself deeper and deeper into the mental states the reader foresaw, which were projected onto you. So then, your karma begins to greatly intertwine with the karma of the fortune-teller, not so much with a personality, but with a mental state that the personality projected to you through the reading. When this occurs, anyone who has a similar mental state, maybe someone at work you never liked or never liked you, begins to seek you out as a companion and, ultimately, bonds karmically with you in some way. So you see, this is how life becomes so compounded and complicated."

Apprentice: "Did you mean anyone as in everyone of that mental state?"

"That's right. All those who carry that mental state, begin to hook up to your destiny, as you go about living your life. So now, you are enlarging your circle of karma, because through your contacts, you are actually linking yourself up to the fortune-tellers particular mental state as it appears in other people. It gets very profoundly complex. So you can see how fortune-telling works against you, and why I would not advise you to participate in it, unless you are as Soul, and if you are living as Soul, you probably would not be interested in asking for a fortune reading. Of course, this kind of karmic bonding occurs because of your confidence in others besides fortune-tellers, as well.

"Someone who lives as Soul can look into another person and perceive the energy there. They do not need to use a divination system to do this, nor does the person unconsciously karmically bond with others. I am not saying that you personally should not use a divination system; but that you do not seek someone to do it for you. Such systems can be useful and they have been used through the ages as a meditative technique, a contemplative technique, but there is a point on the Path of Soul where you move beyond such things, as well.

"Using a divination system for yourself can be used as an indication of where you sit in that moment. If you try to expand your use of divination out of the present moment, to enlarge it into your whole life, you are asking for a complexity that is going to seek out mental states to match it. Be careful, use wisdom. You want to keep yourself as free as possible.

"Astrology is a science. It can tell you about the personality traits you are born with, which means the karmic traits that you were born with. It will also tell you about certain directions and leanings your life will have. Astrology can be a useful tool, but it should never be a binding tool because again, when you begin to tap into the experience of living as Soul, you will transcend the limitation of your astrological chart. You move beyond it, because you will shed much of the karma that forged it. As Soul, you can merge with any sign of the Zodiac. You can be any birthday, any day of the year. (Laughter). You are laughing because many of you have asked me when my birthday is, and I say, *'Oh, when's yours?' 'Oh, well, it's April 28th,'* or some other date, and I say, *'That's mine, too,'* see? Now, I say your birthday is mine as well for a couple of reasons. One is, it doesn't matter when my birthday is, because I can have any birthday I want, and second, if I tell you my birthday and astrologically it is not a compatible sign to you, you will worry about it, and your worry is unnecessary, because I live as Soul, so I can get along with anyone I choose.

"Another thing. Take your ball and chain off. Stop telling people how old you are, or when your birthday is so that they will not have preconceived, rigid ideas about who they think you are. Don't talk about your birthday. Everybody gets born, and everybody dies. What is the big deal? You know, you can be sure we were all born and, at some time, we are all going to die.

"The day you were born is important, but the day you step onto the Path of Soul, is very important. The seed of who you are in the moment you step onto the Path of Soul is a vital energy. It is alive and its energy prods you forward constantly. It is a moment of great power, because its existence has built momentum enough to prod you; to move you forward.

"Your chosen moments in life can be very important; the moment you step onto the Path of Soul, as well as the moment you got married and accepted the karma of another person into your life. The seeds of who you are in the moment of marriage, when you join with another person, is what instigates the fruit of the marriage. It sets a course, a destiny. Later, if your identity of who you were when you married dissipates, because the bond that brought you together has weakened and it can no longer sustain the union, perhaps you have grown beyond it. You will be happy to know that you cannot grow beyond the Path of Soul, because the Path of Soul, unlike an ordinary karmic relationship has no end to it. The Path of Soul is forever expanding outward, unless you have a teacher who stops somewhere on the Path, who becomes comfortable with non-movement. Then that Path also stops; but I promise you, that will not happen here. It really cannot happen on the Path of Soul, because, It has no limit and The Teacher who walks It must also be limitless.

"So take a look at where you are in the moment you begin major steps in your life. When a child is impregnated into your body, your consciousness at that particular moment attracts a the child that will grow in your body. When one gets married, the consciousness that exists between the husband and wife is what is going to make the marriage or break it.

"When people get married because they have a strong physical attraction for each other and not a strong friendship, the marriage most likely will quickly break apart. If a couple comes together because of a great neediness of some kind, such a marriage does not usually last long either. When a person feels secure after feeling needy, there is usually resentment, because now, the needy is strong and wants freedom. They want a partner who accepts them as an equal and the partner who spent so much energy building her or him up, feels more protective than equal. So you kind of take a look at all your situations in life.

"When you meet someone and have the feeling that you instantly know them, you recognize them, you become fast friends. The moment that friendship clicks becomes the energy link of that friendship. So, if you want to know if that friendship will endure, ask yourself what the basis for your friendship is. Some friendships endure separation and, even though you may grow apart for a while, you come back again at another point in life and you are good friends again. Usually these friends are close loving ties from previous lifetimes. You just pick up your friendship at any time where you left off. If, out of the blue you heard that person was in difficulty a thousand miles away, you would jump to the occasion and vice versa. These people are friends forever with you; they never try to tear you down or disrupt your life. They accept you for who you are, which makes them the wealth of your life.

"So, as you can see, divination covers many areas of life and it is filled with intuitive perceptions. Divination systems that are based more directly on your own intuitive power rather than using somebody else's intuitive power, are more valid for you; however, a system is still a system, and anything that is a system is limited by the power and consciousness that gave birth to it, as well as the power and consciousness that uses it. The Tarot has its origins in medieval days but earlier versions existed in many parts of the world. Tibet has many systems of divination, but much of the divination that Tibet uses today has, unfortunately, become tinged with ritual, superstitions and belief systems, like those of other cultures."

Eagle's Presence: "Would you talk about numerology?"

"The Pythagorean theory of numerology is a science that numerically assigns a number to each letter of the alphabet to foretell the vibrations of a word, which are then reduced to a single digit number ranging from 1 to 9, with exceptions of special numbers, in particular 11, 20, 22 and 30. Each of the aforementioned numbers, reflects traits and characteristics that influence a person by name, birthday and activity, as well as relative questions. Entire life cycles can be forecasted through this science, as they are also forecasted through astrology, the I Ching, etc.. But there are some languages that are not reduced to alphabet. The numeral equation then, is very difficult, isn't it?

"A name has power to it according to the moment that it was given to you. If you want to change your name, if you are dissatisfied with what you feel is the moment of power that existed when it came to you, then change it, and whatever influence that occurs around your need to change it, will influence the use of the new name. Furthermore, that influence that you empowered through taking a new name, will be added to your life, so pay attention to why you are doing it.

"A name is like a musical score. The letters are vibrations. When you drop a letter, you drop a musical note, so the name has you appearing differently in vibration. An over abundance of one letter is an over abundance in one vibration. Whatever balance or lack of balance in these vibrations is how you present yourself to the world. Well, I could go on and on, because numerology is an elaborate science, as are most divination systems. The purpose of this talk is not to delve into the heart of each system but to define the common denominators of each and to direct you to effect your own insights within each system, rather than someone else's for reasons explained above.

"Don't limit yourself to a system. The astrological Zodiac is the wheel of karma and you are bound to it only by a rigid consciousness. The same holds true about any divination system. Change your consciousness and throw the dice again. You will get a different answer because you have allowed your mind sets to evolve. So divination can be a useful tool to reset your brain waves, like a biofeedback machine.

"It is interesting to learn about these different things. As a reward, you receive those little flashes of illumination that say, 'Ah-hah;' the *ah-hah state*, the little mental orgasms, you know (laughs). It is exciting, yes, but there is something more exciting than that (a bird squawks outside the Happy House in confirmation). More exciting than that is the radiance of the mind that develops in one who **realizes** God. When the **realization** of God occurs, all books open, all knowledge is open to you. That is one of the gifts of living <u>as</u> Soul, which is your birthright. Why settle for less. You never have to settle for less. I know it is fun to entertain your mind with little ideas of things, and I don't blame you for doing it because, each thing is a stepping stone to the grand realization, only be careful you do not linger too long lest you forget and believe the stepping stone to be more than it is.

"May the blessings be."

"When the realization of God occurs, all books open, all knowledge is open to you."

Steps to Your Destiny

Winged Wolf: "In the primordial teachings, the word *paramita* refers to a quality or set of qualities that makes it possible for an individual to leave one shore and arrive at an opposite shore. It is a good word because to say, *'To arrive at an opposite shore,'* requires more words in English to get the point across.

"Paramita: When you start across a street, it requires that you take a certain amount of steps to reach the opposite curb. Each step is, therefore, profoundly significant; each step accentuates one's direction and leads to the next step. Of course, crossing the street or arriving at an opposite shore is a metaphor for reaching your personal spiritual destiny or destination. There are six basic steps to this accomplishment.

"First is a **giving**, which means a giving of yourself, an openness of yourself, an availability of yourself to do service. And this is very important. No spiritual life can blossom without it. It is in the act of giving that you can receive everything that the spiritual life has to offer, because without giving, you actually close a door and are then unable to receive.

"The second paramita or step is **moral practice**. In other words, you actually practice self-discipline to keep the vows that you have made in life. Whatever vows you make, you make consciously. To break a vow means that the karmic residue of your broken vow will influence the character of your life in the present moment. If you vow fidelity to your spouse, to break that vow places an unsettling feeling between you, even though it is never spoken about with anyone. If you make a promise to a friend, that promise is a vow, and you must keep it. If you gift someone money, you cannot mentally reflect on how wonderful you were for doing it, because to do so is vanity, which is a mind poison that spreads into a barrier between you and the other person. So when you put something out there as a gift to the world, if your vanity is involved, you would be better off to not give, because you surround your good deed with negative karma. When you give with vanity, you silently sit in judgment of the other person, watching how that other person conducts their affairs. Instead, step back. Give and release. All moral practices are to be conducted in this way, by giving and letting go of what you gave, so that you can move on without any further strings of energy attached to you. And I will recommend here; rather than loan money to a friend in need, it is better to give, otherwise you will be waiting for them to pay you back, and in that waiting you will most likely be judgmental. Either you feel yourself testing their integrity or afraid you will not get the return of your money. Don't loan money!

"**Patience**.... Patience is one of those qualities that empowers you to reach the other shore. To rush or to try to bypass the necessary steps it takes to complete a journey, makes the journey incomplete. Every part of the journey is the whole experience of arrival. It is the entire spiritual journey that makes it possible for you to live the teachings. Enjoy the journey.

"The journey never ends. If you do not enjoy this moment, then the fruit that comes out of this moment makes the next moment taste spoiled, as well. Enjoyment of your spiritual journey will light the way for you to recognize the ebb and the flow of life. Patience will assist you to make wise choices, so that you can direct your own course within the flow of the tide. But do not misinterpret the meaning of *going with the flow*. That does not mean that you must go with the flow or the trend. You make your own choices.... always make your own choices.

"The fourth paramita is **effort.** Unfortunately, effort to most people means labor in an uncomfortable way. To many, labor means suffering through something. Please pay attention. It is not necessary to suffer on the spiritual path. If you are suffering most likely you are faced with a karmic debt. Let go of your resistance and much of the suffering will disappear. Effort initiates movement to get you to the other side of the street; you pick one foot up and put it down in front of the other. That is what is meant by effort, not hard labor, not struggle. When you becomes really adept at effort, it becomes effortless. If there is discomfort in your effort you are not enjoying the journey, therefore, you are being impatient. So, relax. Always relax.... When things get tense, relax. Do not allow situations to push or pull you. Push and pull builds into struggle. If you are rushing somewhere and something occurs to slow you down; well, it often means you do not have to rush.... there is plenty of time at the other end. Relax.

"The fifth paramita quality necessary to reaching your spiritual shore is learning to **sit in the silence,** which not only quiets you down from the activities of the day and removes you from busyness, it is food for Soul. It strengthens Soul's presence in your total life, which empowers you and makes your mind brilliant. The best ideas and solutions always result from a period of sitting in the silence, so sitting in the silence is the pot of gold everyone seeks. Another gift of the silence is joy and a sense of unrestrained freedom, which is the nature of Soul. Soul is naturally happy. If you are unhappy, a sure solution is to acquire the skill of sitting in the silence. It gives you the power to reach any destination, your physical goals, including abundance in business, because with Soul in command of your life, all the push/pull and conflicting thoughts are removed so that you can operate at peak performance. You naturally have patience to succeed, and you are not so caught up and attached to the results.

"And the sixth paramita is **wisdom**. You have to pay attention to what the moment calls for, and to give it that. If you are unaware of what you are doing, unaware of your actions, unaware of your speech, unaware of your thoughts, unaware of your energy and what you are putting out into the environment, your energy will disrupt others, as well as the flow of your own life. So if you are out there pounding around on your bongos, (speaking to an apprentice who visited the property with her bongos) totally oblivious to everything and not conscious of what you are doing, then you are not using wisdom, unless you are in an environment where it is totally acceptable. Being aware means that you are not asleep; therefore, you can exercise the wisdom that is required for the given moment, the given situation.

"May the blessings be."

"Let go of your resistance and much of the suffering will disappear."

Experiencing Unwavering Centeredness
(without Delusion)

Winged Wolf: "Please pay attention, very careful attention.

"The construction of life, ideas and object creations are already finished. In other words, life is already a '*done deal.*' All things in life are already completed; there is nothing new, nor can there be anything new. Anything that you or I or someone else envisions, an idea and/or an ideal already exists, which is why, when you are aware of yourself as Soul, the manifestation of objects sometimes seems little more than slight of hand, a little effort and presto: The realization of matter occurs when urgency strikes the canvas of desire, which ignites the God-force into action.

"Everything is already here, yet hidden, waiting to become manifest, to spring forth from the *natural state* that exists in you already. When you **realize** the natural state, and **realize** is a condition of awareness that exceeds the intellectual, you have begun to grasp the God Consciousness. So you can see, unwavering centeredness reveals the depth of who you have become, and awakens you to the clarity of your relationship with all life. The clarity of your special relationship with all life is a humbling yet glorious experience, because now you become a servant of God, the Void. And, in so doing, you claim the throne of power, as you, yourself, stake claim as the monarch of life, a servant for God as God, the Void.

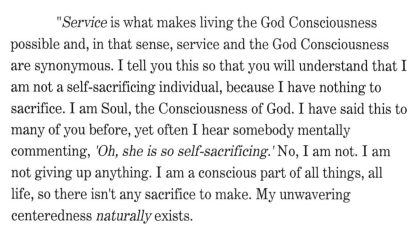

"*Service* is what makes living the God Consciousness possible and, in that sense, service and the God Consciousness are synonymous. I tell you this so that you will understand that I am not a self-sacrificing individual, because I have nothing to sacrifice. I am Soul, the Consciousness of God. I have said this to many of you before, yet often I hear somebody mentally commenting, *'Oh, she is so self-sacrificing.'* No, I am not. I am not giving up anything. I am a conscious part of all things, all life, so there isn't any sacrifice to make. My unwavering centeredness *naturally* exists.

"This does not mean that I don't get tired. Some of the fantasies being acted out here are in horror story form, which is very tiring, (Speaking about apprentices who visit the property to work with The Teacher), yet worthwhile because, gradually, a little more light comes into each of you everyday.

`"Unwavering centeredness comes to one who is in a relaxed state, so get really comfortable, not pseudo-comfortable, but comfortable at being impeccable. The God Consciousness lives in joy, so there is enjoyment in the moment, whatever the moment brings."

Loving Crow: As I am starting to understand, I see one dimensionally; that is, I see the past, the present, and the future and, as something comes up, I process it in this way. How does one go beyond seeing life in this way?"

"Of the past?"

Loving Crow: "Of looking at things from the past or projecting the future?"

"Drop your idea of the past and drop your idea of the future. Instead live in the present where they both exist."

Wings of Change: "About getting thrown out of balance.... You said something like 'chasing glimmers will throw you out of balance'."

"Sometimes, if you chase a glimmer (of understanding) ... you pull, you pinch it off, by your intensity to hold it."

Wings of Change: "So I have a moment of insight, and then I want more of that, and I try to get it by manipulating the situation."

"Yes. You cannot manipulate a situation and come out ahead, because a manipulator becomes the manipulated. That is why I asked you last night (looking at Loving Crow), when you wanted to write about your great discovery.... to leave it alone. Relax. Read a book instead, or go outside to look at the stars, do you see? Turn on something silly on the television - anything to get yourself to relax, because if you get in there to dig at it, the realization pinches off. Now you know why, when you were so intense, I asked you to pick blades of grass, to shift your attention. I was trying to get you to laugh a little bit, rather than getting hung up in your discoveries. It is the integration of what you discover while living life, that empowers you. Life is the tool."

Wings of Change: "I am still thinking about chasing glimmers, and was wondering if there is an element of trust involved in chasing glimmers? Sometimes, when I get a glimmer, I don't have faith that, if I let it go and relax, it will continue to evolve in me. It is like, I have to have it now because it might never come back."

"Yes, well that is what Loving Crow was talking about last night. She said, *'Well, if I don't write, I will lose it.'* I'm saying, *No, you won't lose it.* You will only lose it if you try to grab at it, then your realization dissipates into an intellectual mulling over, and then you will lose it or detain it for awhile. Don't do that. Relax. Go outside and mow the lawn with your fingers. Pick one blade of grass at a time. You know, people who are really far along the spiritual Path appear a little *crackers* sometimes. They do silly things like that. They may watch the grass grow, or they pick the grass one blade at a time instead of mowing it, simply to shift their intensity to relaxation, not because they are really mowing the lawn that way.

"Give up thinking that you have to be programmed into doing something to occupy yourself all the time. Your reply to my encouragement to move about outside was (looking at Loving Crow), <u>was</u>, *'Well, then I will get on the Internet.'* Why jumble yourself up by busying yourself so you don't think? Do things that help you relax instead, so that the glimmers can grow. Glimmers grow in relaxation. Glimmers of spiritual light grow in you through your relaxation."

Loving Crow: "You know, it wasn't intellectual when it came."

"Of course not."

Loving Crow: "It just came. Something you had been saying...."

"But you wanted to intellectualize it then."

Loving Crow: "Well, because I tried to intellectualize..."

"I am going to write a paper for Stanford University', (referring to the comment Loving Crow told Winged Wolf the night before).

(There is much laughter)

"Why do you have to get your ego involved in it?"

Loving Crow: "Maybe I could help others."

"Forget about impressing others with your knowledge and just take care of yourself. Develop yourself and then you will naturally assist others by your readiness. I don't know if you heard that."

Loving Crow: "I heard it."

"You run off to help others, and you are only going to make a big mess of things, because you are not taking care of what you need to take care of first, and that is your own spiritual life.
"May the blessings be."

"Give up thinking that you have to be programmed into doing something to occupy yourself all the time."

The Five Eyes

Winged Wolf: "This talk is something that I wrote down, and probably the title seems oddball like. I call it *The Five Eyes.* (quiet laughter) That gives everybody the impression of five eyeballs and I did not quite mean it like that. I meant more like the five different types of vision.

"The first type of vision is the **physical eye** vision where we're able to see the manifested illusions around us and those manifested illusions move and transmute into other energies to become other things. For instance, you can see a car drive down the street; you can see the making of a piece of clay into a statue, do you see. So you can see the movement of things and the transmutation of energies through movement. So the power of the physical eyes or the vision of the physical eyes, which is quite special in itself, is to perceive movement and to perceive the illusion that is propelled through the movement of sentient beings, as well as the transmutation of their energy into other things. So to say, *'Oh well that's physical'*.... take another look, it is pretty special in itself.

"The second type of eye that I put down there was the **divine eye,** the eye that looks through the heart and is able to see the simplicity of the illusion itself of the physical world. It is able to acknowledge love and compassion for what is being seen. The transmutation of energy can be a positive transmutation or it can be a negative transmutation of someone's life. With this type of vision, you can see someone being injured by energy, as well as someone being healed by it. The divine eye can discern the difference between the two and continue to love in a divine sense, which is also compassion in order to assist the energy that is out

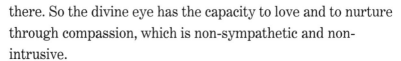

there. So the divine eye has the capacity to love and to nurture through compassion, which is non-sympathetic and non-intrusive.

"And then we have the third eye, the **wisdom eye**. The wisdom eye is the eye that takes what it knows and it practices that, so whatever the individual knows is then put into use within the environment. So the physical eye and the divine eye can use the wisdom eye to refine what the physical eye is seeing, do you see. And it can also help transmute that energy in an uplifting way. And, transmuting energy in an uplifting way can only come about through wisdom, because wisdom is a state of correct choice, correct not being right or wrong as most people speak of it, but correct meaning the choice of going in the direction of what you want, rather than what you do not want. Most people live according to what they do not want because they feel that is what is expected of them. When one begins to live the division of the wisdom eye, they begin to make choices that benefit them, enhancing what it is that they want to do.

"And then we have the fourth eye, the **eye of the teaching**. The teaching in itself is primordial. It goes back to the beginning of time, and it has a vision or a viewpoint that it projects that is all encompassing of all the other visions that we spoke of. The teaching eye incorporates all physical vision. It sees what can be and what is, and it also has the power to dictate various means of transmutation of the energy that is perceived, because the transmutation in itself becomes the teaching. The teaching is not a stagnant or a dead thing written on paper. This is where people become confused. The teaching itself, since it is primordial, means that it has the power and impetus behind it to actually extend its energy into life forms. You see, even if someone makes a choice that is negative or not uplifting to them, that is still a part of the teaching, only it is a division of the teaching rather than the whole.

"So the eye of the teaching sees the dualities; you know, the plus and the minus, the pro and the con, the good and the bad, the light and the dark, the rain and the sunshine. It sees all the dualities and it extends a lightness of life into the vibration in all that it teaches. And in the vibration that is extended outward, it has first a life-force of its own because it is the primordial teaching....it is that it is. IT IS! It is the primordial life-force upon which all of life exists. It is the life-force of the wisdom eye, the divine eye and the physical eye. It is all of that. So therefore, this eye of the teaching is actually the life-force behind all other vision. This is what makes all vision possible. The primordial teachings exist as a reality, not as a text of knowledge, although it can be written down in a book of knowledge. However, the book of knowledge can only penetrate a person to the extent of their openness to receive it. Although in the hearing of the primordial knowledge, the openness that an individual has resonates in them and therefore the opening gets bigger.

"Now my reason in telling you these things about the five different eyes is to help you understand how life expands; how your choice comes into action, so that you can recognize the impact of your choices upon your empowerment.

"The fifth eye is the **enlightened eye**. Since the primordial teachings have set the foundation for all the eyes, so the teaching is the power of all eyes. All of them are what makes it possible to see with the physical eyes, the divine eye and the wisdom eye, the primordial teachings being the oneness of all things. The enlightened eye is the one that perceives all the other four eyes. It is the one that first recognizes and then *realizes* what the eye of the teaching is about; what the wisdom eye does for an individual, and what the divine eye does for all sentient beings. The divine eye is the healer, you see, because it gives divine love and compassion. It is the healing eye. And the physical eye has the magnificent power of actually glimpsing the illusion itself in manifested form. How powerful sight is!

"So, those are a few little things that I wanted to pass on to you.... little nuggets so that you can see how your own life-force interacts with the primordial teachings, which is really what we are talking about.

"The enlightened eye is only the perceiver of everything that I have mentioned. That is all it is. It is the perceiver and the realizer. It is the eye that realizes the connection between the physical eye, the divine eye, the wisdom eye and the teaching eye. As the realizer, it is the vision of life that is able to consciously act out what it knows.

"Sometimes it helps to have things broken apart so that you can see how the bits and pieces of things interlock with each other; so that you can recognize the magnificent power of the physical eye, and not take it for granted. It is through recognition that realization comes to pass, so if you want to use the enlightened eye, you must first recognize the world in which you live and what you have propelled through your own mental imagery, the illusion that has become hardened matter. You begin to see things. Now, when you begin to see life and how energy exists; when you wish for things and they come to pass, then you can also witness the transmutation of those same energies into becoming something else, you know. In other words, when your wishes are fulfilled, they begin to evolve into something else. Through this transmutation, you can begin to see the choices you have made and their effects. You begin to

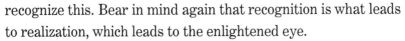

recognize this. Bear in mind again that recognition is what leads to realization, which leads to the enlightened eye.

"So, as you recognize your choices, you also recognize that your choices bring the results that you want and other choices bring the results that you do not want. Eventually, you will stop choosing what you do not want, which then develops the wisdom eye through that action, do you see? Through right action you develop the wisdom eye and you begin then, through the wisdom eye, of choosing what you want rather than what you do not want or what everybody else tells you you have to have. You are then living impeccably, and wisdom begins to propel your life with a great and magnificent force. And that great force awakens you to how life actually works. Through the wisdom eye you have dared to be impeccable, do you see? And through your daring to be impeccable, you now come to realize or to recognize the primordial precept that underlies the principles that underlie all life.

"When you recognize this, you begin to see solutions to your life problems and you begin to consciously work with the primordial teaching itself. Through your recognition and through the test you put upon your recognition, you view results that are spiritual law. You live through the eye of the teaching and it dictates your life for you, because you know how to flow in and out with it. You are becoming truly empowered at that point.

"Now, when you become truly empowered, something else happens. Through all this recognition that you are gaining, you are gaining the realization of your recognition. You begin to recognize yourself as Soul and the part of the God-force that makes the primordial teachings alive in your life. And now you begin to live the enlightened eye. And that is when real life begins, a real zest for life, a real excitement in living life, because

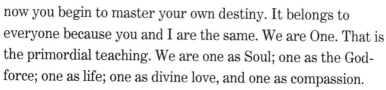

now you begin to master your own destiny. It belongs to everyone because you and I are the same. We are One. That is the primordial teaching. We are one as Soul; one as the God-force; one as life; one as divine love, and one as compassion.

"May the blessings be."

"It is through recognition that realization comes to pass, so if you want to use the enlightened eye, you must first recognize the world in which you live and what you have propelled through your own mental imagery, the illusion that has become hardened matter."

Stillness

Winged Wolf: "The greatest relief for your stress in life is to become unified with the stillness that exists when you put your attention on the Third Eye. If you will take time for yourself everyday to be absolutely quiet for one hour a day, your life will begin the shift to change into being what you would like it to be.... in every way. *Being absolutely quiet* means that during your hour of quiet time, you are not reading, not watching television, not talking to somebody, not entertaining yourself in any way. To do this properly, it would help to spend your hour sitting up straight in an unupholstered chair, feet flat on the floor; or better yet, sit cross-legged on a cushion on the floor, your back perfectly straight. Put your attention on the Third Eye. Every time your attention wanders, catch it and refocus on the center of your forehead (Third Eye). It will get easier as you go along.

"By being still one hour a day, you will gain a great inner strength, a strength that will take you through anything. Also, in that stillness, you will gain power, a power to achieve what you want out of life. The power we speak of has many names. We know It as divine love, a power developed in the stillness that has remarkable capacities to It, capacities that may be beyond your present imagination.

"It is okay to have images flowing through your mind, while in the stillness, but make an effort to not get caught up in mind-chatter or thoughts in words. When the word chatter starts in your mind, realize that your mind is tense and that your mental tension is responsible for the words that are thought-spoken. Just relax. As images present themselves, look at the images and allow them to pass, instead of dwelling on them. If you dwell on them, then your attention locks onto the image and, words will start to chatter in your mind. So, do not freeze your attention on an image. Look at it and continue to look at it, as though you were flipping the pages of a picture book, watching a stream of pictures float past you. If you can stay away from analyzing what you are seeing, the stillness of detached observation will keep you centered at the Third Eye. When you develop a sensibility within the stillness, there is little you will not be able to do."

(There is a very long pause as Winged Wolf looks at each apprentice.)

"One hour a day in the stillness. One hour a day. You are going to have to carve that time out of your day yourself. No one is going to give it to you. Your families are not going to give it to you, because they will want your attention, especially at that time. So you are going to have to set a time when you are not to be disturbed. If you do it everyday at the same time, it will make it easier, because your family will get used to it, but if you cannot do it everyday at the same time, it is okay too. Early morning and/or early evening at the approximate same time makes for a good habit, like you have an approximate set time to brush your teeth.

"It is best in the beginning, if you cannot sit an hour, to sit for a half-hour, and during the day, or early evening sit in the silence another half-hour.

"May the blessings be."

Listening to Space

Winged Wolf: "Listen. There is silence within the silence.... As you talk, as you hear an airplane overhead, or a crow caw, if you pay careful attention, you will become aware of little spaces in-between the sounds. It is those little spaces in-between, that you want to seek out. The little spaces in-between sound is the silence you are looking for, and those spaces of silence can come alive when you pay attention to them. The silence you hear may make outside sounds seem more noticeably louder, but all the same, by listening in this way you may *realize* the true nature of sound.

"While you are listening to the silence, and you hear a sound, and you perceive the energy of that sound, you can recognize what such energy conveys. This is very important, because this state of consciousness is also your sanctuary; you are totally safe as long as you are listening to the silence.

"Through listening to the silence, *you can realize* the energy going on in circumstances around you, via observation, and I mean observation of the silence between sounds. There is a very intricate little hole, a very intricate little space there, which I will call a hole between sounds.

"As I am speaking, the crystal bowl in this room is echoing slightly, and in-between the echo there is a minuscule pocket of silence. There is a pocket of silence between each word that I am speaking now, and if you are observing the pocket of silence, you can truly gain what it is that I am telling you.

"The manner in which I am speaking, the words I am saying also have little pockets of space within them. Do you sense it? Pay keen attention to these pockets of space. They are little holes in space. These holes are avenues into the Void (God). When you put your attention on them you are plugged into the Void. It is this connection that links your Consciousness to the Void.

"And so, all that energy from the Void flows into you so that you can comprehend this, not through analyzation but through a comprehension that is akin to knowingness. However, it is not really a knowingness either, because *knowingness* can sometimes manifest from grabbing at concepts or ideas, like a flash of inspiration or something. Well, we are talking about a comprehension that is more than that. We are talking about an *avenue*, a direct relationship into the Void, which can be perceived only by contact within the pockets of silence.

"This is why I say to you, Listen. Get to the edge of your energy capsule until you feel it. Push your energy against your skin so that you can perceive what is around you, because when you live like that, when you live on the edge, when you live as if you are always listening, you are plugged into the spaces between sounds.

"Now, this is very exciting, because when you get plugged into these spaces between sounds, something happens. You are consciously plugged into the Void (God), so you know that *whatever* you experience is going to be from the Void, and not illusionary.

"The Void will fill you as you listen, and as the Void fills you, you will gain a particular energy. You are connected to the source. You can carry divine energy into the next incident in your life without thinking or conjuring It into being. If you think about It or intellectualize over it, you cut It off; you disconnect. But if you proceed to the next incident in your life, you still have the connection. You continue to listen to the little pockets as you continue your life, you see? And then the experience expands, and you become more and more of the Void Itself, because you are becoming filled with It.

"Gradually, you begin to understand, then you begin to recognize more than understand; to recognize when you are connected and when you are not. Life then becomes very simple to live.

"Listen. Push your energy to the edge of your skin but do not push it beyond. You have to contain your energy. Spend your days listening. Listen keenly, as if you are expecting something, but without expectations, merely have an attitude of listening about you. (Winged Wolf looks around the room at each apprentice and slowly says,) This is why I ask you to spend most of your days in silence when you are here with me.

"Too much useless talk preoccupies your mind so that you forget to listen to the silence. As you move to do a task, do it deliberately, and do not waste movement. Do not use body movements that have no meaning. Be deliberate. This way you will be tuned into the spaces within movement, the spaces within sound. Remember, movement is sound. Movement is sound in motion, an interpretation of the same vibratory rate.

"So, pay attention to the movements you have. Be frugal with them. Let the power of silence build in you. Let the Void build in you. The Void is *the* power. The Void is God. Do not squander. Know what you are doing, and as you listen to those little pockets of silence, you will come to understand all energy. What a gift this is.... becoming One with the Void.

"As you become One with the Void, you also get to know It. You get to know the Void through becoming One with It. What we are speaking about is God Realization. This is what *Recognizing God* is all about. First you recognize what God is and then, gradually, you will realize God. It is a very simple teaching, but not necessarily easy. You can grasp it this moment, and then it may elude you for awhile. You are grasping it through me, you see. You are a part of my consciousness right now and so you are realizing It through my consciousness.

"When you go out into the world, away from me, you will carry a little bit of energy from it with you. You will recall the energy of this interlude, even though it will not have a name. It will not have words connected to it.... Remember to listen to the spaces between the sound. As a bird chirps, in-between the chirp, there is a pause. Listen for it."

Easy Walker: "Well, I have just one question. I don't even know if it is related but you were talking about paying attention to the spaces between. The other day you mentioned a bubble, and you said you were riding the bubble. I don't know what a bubble is to tell you the truth. Is that connecting to the space between?"

"A bubble is an energy field, which has a light and sound energy field, which every person also has. It is the aura of a person. You are sitting here in your bubble. Your energy field is contained around you because you are not pushing your energy out. The idea is to never push your energy out. You get in other people's space when you do that. Stay to yourself. That way all of life is yours. *You are all of life.*

"So, what you can do with this bubble that is around you, is to move it. You are actually moving your body to move your energy, just like exercising a muscle or stretching a muscle. There are many variations to the same thing, you see. And as you learn the variations of the HÜM mantra, then you will learn that there are unlimited capabilities of being One with the Void. The Void is always becoming; there is no end to it. God, the Void, is ever expansive.

"The whole purpose of life is to consciously express the God force into the world; to express the Void into the world. What a gift. It makes life exceedingly joyful and exceedingly rewarding; not that it doesn't have its painful moments. It does, usually when someone near you is in pain, and out of compassion you stand by them with love. You can just be there.

"May the blessings be."

".... when you get plugged into these spaces between sounds, something happens. You are consciously plugged into the Void (God), so you know that whatever you experience is going to be from the Void, and not illusionary."

Ocean of Silence

Winged Wolf: "To hear the silence means to be able to listen to the silence. To listen means to have your mind quiet so that you can observe sights, feel the vibrations and hear the ultimate stillness. If you look out of yourself in this way, then you can have the experience of being a part of the ocean of silence, which exists within the heart of God. To be still, means that you have no expectations about the experiences that you evoke nor any other preconceived ideas about the nature of silence. Being *still* means you will be flexible in the moment so that you do not have any assumption about it at all. In other words, the silence is primordially present, and you are primordially present with it, as well. When you allow this state to exist in your consciousness, you can truly *hear* because you are perceiving the silence, Itself.

"Please listen carefully. We are not talking about an ordinary way of hearing, although the ordinary sense of hearing can be affected by the subject we are discussing.

"When a person loses their hearing, or is born deaf, it is oftentimes because, somewhere along their lifetime(s), the person stopped listening to the silence. Silence may have become fearful, because one's mind suddenly exaggerated images of aloneness and isolation. In this sense, silence can become deafening. Sometimes people listen to loud sounds or loud music to ease feelings of aloneness and isolation. Becoming deaf can also result from a sudden shock, or sustained shock, sustained feelings of belittlement, or unhappiness, fear, extreme discomfort, or other traumatic upsets that tend to cause a person to block out, or shut down their sense of hearing to become deaf. How can sound return to deaf ears? The cause must be removed

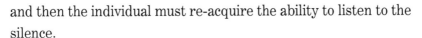
and then the individual must re-acquire the ability to listen to the silence.

"As an example, Skywolf (an apprentice) was born deaf, a deafness that was caused in a previous lifetime. Now, through his daily spiritual practices of sitting in the silence these last two years, he is beginning to hear. The low pitch sounds are returning to him and he has now, at age 40+, graduated to a hearing aid. He can even hear the flap of a crow's wings as it flies overhead, among many other wonderful sounds.

"To re-acquire the ability to hear, one must spend time sitting in the silence, listening to the silence, until they become aware that, even in silence, there are *particular,* otherwise unnoticed sounds, born from the motion of atoms and molecules, stirred by powerful vibrations from the Void Itself. This awareness is gradual and individual. It begins, when the person no longer struggles against silence and accepts it; then, bit-by-bit, his attention brings about an awareness of vibrations."

Easy Walker: "I don't even know what to ask you."

"In the stillness, there is a diffusion of sight, just as there is a diffusion of sound, just as there is a diffusion of your feelings, which is why, when that occurs, you have no questions. It is interesting to note that the diffusion we now speak of is really soft-eyed vision, or peripheral visioning, or what we speak of as Soul Vision. When in Soul Vision, tension as we ordinarily think of it does not exist; the mind perceives rather than questions. In other words, everything is visibly soft to the eyes, which makes the moment questionless. However, when you resort back into hard-focus, you will resort to uncertainty again, and questions will naturally appear.

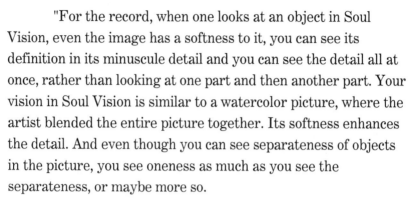

"For the record, when one looks at an object in Soul Vision, even the image has a softness to it, you can see its definition in its minuscule detail and you can see the detail all at once, rather than looking at one part and then another part. Your vision in Soul Vision is similar to a watercolor picture, where the artist blended the entire picture together. Its softness enhances the detail. And even though you can see separateness of objects in the picture, you see oneness as much as you see the separateness, or maybe more so.

"So, consider this. When life becomes segmented to you, it becomes filled with questions. When life becomes little slices of the whole, it is suddenly filled with questions, and doubts, and conflicts. But if you put it back into the pie, that slice becomes one with the whole. To perceive the energy of what you are looking at, look at the whole pie, not a separate slice.

"The individual who takes a drop of water to study the ocean, does not really understand the ocean, even though the drop of water has all the components of the ocean, including its fluidity. Such a person is looking at a little droplet of the ocean, that is all.

"Everyday, seven days a week, I give the teachings out. If someone hears one teaching and says, *'Yes, this is the whole teaching.'* Well yes, it is, in a way.... It is a slice of the pie; a drop of water from the ocean. And that person may take that teaching and sincerely integrate it into their lives, believing it to be the whole. And, I would have to agree, it is the whole; but it is not the whole, as well, because the person is firmly focused on only a little droplet .

"The Teachings of Soul are so vast that there is no end to them. They are so clear that you can see forever through them, which is why you take that one little drop and you say, *'I can see forever through it.'* And indeed you can! But it is still not the whole, because as you are staring at perhaps one or two or three little drops of water; you become so caught up with the fact that you know all of life because you know the drops of water that you forget that it is only a very small portion of the great ocean of divinity.

"I have said many times before that each step of the consciousness that you acquire is only the beginning. And that is all it is. I may see the ocean, but what I see is still only a beginning for me, as well. Sometimes it upsets people when I say this, because they feel that the beginning is a lowly place, which is not true. The beginning is an eternity that has no end to it, yet it is constantly enriching our lives. As I look at your faces, I reflect on your lives and how they have blossomed since you have begun on the Path of Soul.

"You received a little drop of water and then another and another, ongoing. It is still only one drop because all the droplets merged. My droplet is continually growing in size. I keep adding drops, you see? You, too, may have many drops of water now; but maybe not the ocean, as yet. You may not have a cupful, but there are still many drops to add. Don't confuse yourself by saying that you have all you need, or have *all of it*, because you do not have all of it. I do not have all of it either. My spiritual teacher did not have all of it. No Teacher has ever had all of it.

"The Void (God) is always expanding. As you take on a new droplet of water, the Void expands. There is no end to it. It is vanity to think that you have achieved the ultimate; or that you know it all; or that you don't need any more droplets of water, because the droplets that you have contain everything. Indeed they do, but you will get lost in what you have. You will lose the significance of the greater whole. And you need a resource to

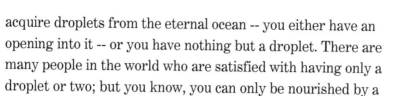

acquire droplets from the eternal ocean -- you either have an opening into it -- or you have nothing but a droplet. There are many people in the world who are satisfied with having only a droplet or two; but you know, you can only be nourished by a droplet so long, and then it evaporates into nothing.

"The ocean of the Teachings is endless. It will never dry up. There is always so much more. You will never come to a point of 'Ho-hum, I know it all,' and this fact makes life very exciting, very clear, very pristine, very enriching. It makes it a joy to be alive. You can never get bored.

"The tiredness that you may gain from extending yourself in service, assisting others on the Path, is a superficial tiredness. It is easy to rejuvenate yourself, because you are constantly moving forward; you are constantly ingesting the teachings. After a while, the teachings become YOU; you become the ocean of the Void, and whatever you want to know comes flowing out of you. Every time you open your mouth, the pump is activated. Every time you look at something, the pump is activated. Every time you hear something or smell something or touch something, the pump is activated. Your body becomes a true sensory machine -- to activate the source -- and you need your body to activate that source, because it is your body's senses that activate the source. You must, however, keep your body as healthy and strong as you can. Take care of it.

"And when you sit still, looking out of your body, listening to the silence and smelling the clear or the stale air, it doesn't matter, the Void is activated into that as well....because your body is the pump....your brain is the pump, and it produces images that always lubricate the pump. It is endless....forever.

"As Soul, you are living your most potent moment, a moment that goes on forever. You are beyond caring about

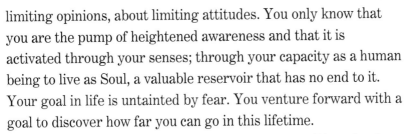

limiting opinions, about limiting attitudes. You only know that you are the pump of heightened awareness and that it is activated through your senses; through your capacity as a human being to live as Soul, a valuable reservoir that has no end to it. Your goal in life is untainted by fear. You venture forward with a goal to discover how far you can go in this lifetime.

"It all goes back to listening to the silence. Listening is about feeling the vibrations of life, of which sound is a part. There is a smoothness to silence and there's an agitation to it, and the agitation has different textures, just like the smoothness has different textures.

"Touch upon the silence and get to know what that silence feels like. When it ripples in agitation, recognize that the vibration is about to change into something you can see and/or hear on the physical plane. It is matter becoming manifest. Agitation is required to manifest new situations. The agitation is vibrant movement. In other words, when vibration is agitated in a certain way, it manifests. This is a law of physics and it has nothing to do with good or bad manifestation. Your mind stuff will predict that. When you come to grips with this, you can learn the art of *presenting* your own life as you want it to be.

"Listen to the silence and the silence between the silences.... between the sounds....Pay attention to the silence between sounds. As your breath moves, there are moments in-between, little split seconds of silence, as your lungs fill up, before they exhale. Do you see?

"Listen to the silence, that is where your ocean is; that is how you will tap its resources. That is how you will become the pump into the ocean of the Void, by recognizing the silence, by watching that silence churn and move and agitate and vibrate,

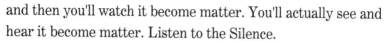

and then you'll watch it become matter. You'll actually see and hear it become matter. Listen to the Silence.

"May the blessings be!"

"When life becomes segmented to you, it becomes filled with questions. When life becomes little slices of the whole, it is suddenly filled with questions, and doubts, and conflicts. But if you put it back into the pie, that slice becomes one with the whole. To perceive the energy of what you are looking at, look at the whole pie, not a separate slice."

Mental States

Winged Wolf: "I saw a photograph of three women, representing three generations - one a woman in her mid- eighties; her daughter some twenty years younger and the daughter's daughter probably some twenty years younger than her mother, as well. There was a resemblance in all three faces, and a resemblance in their bodies. They did not look alike actually, but there was a *look* about them that was the same. The similarity I speak of was not brought about by outward appearances alone, but by a mental state that each shared that made them look alike.

"Interestingly enough, the mental states each shared were brought about by their resistance toward each other; they constantly fought each other. One fought the mental state of the other. The daughter resisted the mental states of her mother and became just like her. The daughter resented her mother's scrutinization of others and yet she did exactly the same thing, putting her mother at the top of her scrutinization list. They shared that same trait or mental state, which resulted in the daughter unconsciously copying her mother's expressions, and these expressions were responsible for making them *look alikes*, in the same way stage performers, who are imitators, are adept at copying expressions, giving the appearance of the one being imitated.

"The daughters and mothers shared more than a single attitude together; they shared many attitudes and opinions about things. What they shared were not always negative opinions; they shared positive opinions, as well, although the daughter fought and belittled her mother for having them. Yet, interestingly enough, when the daughter was not with the mother, she expressed herself in exactly the same way her

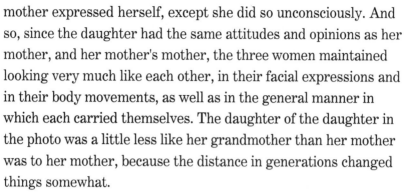

mother expressed herself, except she did so unconsciously. And so, since the daughter had the same attitudes and opinions as her mother, and her mother's mother, the three women maintained looking very much like each other, in their facial expressions and in their body movements, as well as in the general manner in which each carried themselves. The daughter of the daughter in the photo was a little less like her grandmother than her mother was to her mother, because the distance in generations changed things somewhat.

"You can see people on the street who have a timid demeanor, yet there is a strength to their face, a presence to them. Twenty years ago if you were to see somebody like that, they would have been a meek-looking individual. But because of the mental state they are carrying, their face takes on a look of strength, whereas otherwise, it would look weak. Their mental states have empowered them.

"There again, someone who is a really nice-looking person, can have a meek look about them, shifty eyes, and an uncertain way of carrying their body. That is their mental state showing through.

"Now, people who have changed so drastically since they have come into their body, often look like they are wearing masks, because their bodies and their minds do not seem to fit. Their bodies still have to evolve to catch up to where they are, and they will. Next time they will have the same kind of look, but their body will have evolved slightly to match their evolution.... Life is so simple. To become it, you simply fuse with it. You were raised with parents and you naturally fused with their opinions, attitudes and mental states. It is very natural.

"Little children are like parrots. Whatever their parents say they repeat, and sometimes they do not even know what they are repeating. They grow up and they are still repeating the same thing. Gradually they catch on to the meaning of it and they begin to think, *'Well, now, what is this?'* It is like a child going to catechism in a Catholic school. He is taught repetitive words.

"All of a sudden one day in later life, age twenty-two or so, he is saying the words and he suddenly says, *'Oh, what am I saying? Is that what I'm saying?'* And he begins to have an understanding of the words themselves. Then he has to decide, they either have a meaning that he wants to keep or he must discard them. If he discards them, his mental state changes. If he keeps them, his mental state changes as well, because he knows the meaning of what he is saying. Either way is fine.

"As long as he acts repetitively, while living in the environment, and as long as he acts like his parents without being aware of it, he is asleep, hypnotized in consciousness. As a result, he maintains the mental states of his parents. He will have all of their problems and all of their types of enjoyment.. His life is a carbon copy.

"The Path of Soul wakes you up to who you are, you as Soul. *'Who are you?'* I know who you are. There are a couple of you I have to take a hammer and chisel to, to try to crack you open just enough so that you can see a tiny bit of who you are. What I am saying here is that each person, for the most part, is a composite of their parents: You are your mother; you are your father, and you are also what you have made of being a part of the two put together.... or, one plus one equals three; you being the third party.

"If, indeed, you carried none of the same mental states as those in your family, you would look quite different. You see this occasionally in siblings. There may be one sibling who looks totally different and out of sorts with the rest of the family. This is because for some reason or another, he or she does not carry the family's mental states. Karmically, the bond is altered. Somehow or another, the child slipped through the barriers of physical life, not through like attraction but through opposite attraction. It is a quirk of destiny that sometimes comes to pass. Soul literally found an empty wound and crawled into it to gain entrance into a physical body. Such a child lives in the family but is not of it.

"This next part is very important, so please pay close attention. You can never break away from a mental state if you are resisting it. If you are resisting it, you strengthen your bond with it. If you want to be different from your parents, do not resist them. Do not find fault with them, because what you find fault with, you are. By this I mean that, in resistance, one uses the mental state he is resistant to, to present conflict. In other words, you present a mirror image to battle the original image; therefore, you are reflecting that same mental state. Instead, accept your parents for who they are. Love them unconditionally, divinely. This type of love does not mean that you necessarily like what another person does, simply that, you love them as Soul. When you are capable of loving another as Soul, then you consciously become more and more Soul or divine-like. In this way, you are brought closer together and yet more distant in temperaments, which means you look less and less like your parents.

"The other day I was in a shop in town. One of my apprentices came in and a man who was there, asked if we were related. Of course, we don't look at all alike, but the apprentice carries many of my mental states, it seemed that we were related; which, in a sense, we are. So, what you put your attention upon, you become.

"People sometimes fear diseases that tend to run in their families. I have an apprentice who was very concerned because her mother and grandmother died of the same disease and so it went all through her family. She said, *I'm scared to death that I'm going to be next.'*

"I explained to her that she does not have to be next, if she is willing to break away from the mental state that propagated the disease. The disease will actually be eliminated from her genes, because it was only held in place by long-term family attitudes. Can you see what I am saying? You have heard the expression, *'You are what you eat.'* In like expression, *'You are what you think.'* It's that simple. Just because there is a tendency toward developing a particular disease in your family, does not mean that it has to become a part of your life.

"If you are centered as Soul, everything will be working for you; you will be removed from the victim of circumstances realm. I am telling you, you are not trapped by someone else's mental state unless you allow it. You are not locked into accepting anything you do not want in your life. Even a deformity that is passed on from generation to generation, such as, *'My grandmother had it, so I have it.'* You carry that part of your grandmother in yourself. All you have to do is discover what that unwanted link is that you are carrying and discard it. Then you no longer have it.

"Now, I know you have questions arising in you, but if you can hold your minds quiet, then I can tell you more. When your minds are busy, then the words I speak try to answer the questions forming in your minds, rather than the information you really need to hear. Share the mental state that I carry as Soul and you can share my union with the Void. Stay with me.

"As you learn to live as Soul, you will develop the capability to learn from the mental states of others. For instance, if you want to know what it is like to be a great scientist, then fuse your mentality with that mentality. Make a great study of someone like Einstein. Get to know everything about him, the way he walked, the way he moved, the things that he said, his expressions. As you begin to pay attention to those expressions, attitudes and opinions that he carried within himself, you will take them on. As you do so, you will be walking in his mentality. You, too, will have the type of mind that he had. The Sioux Native Americans call this practice *Shanunpa.* It means to fuse with the life force of an animal or a human for the purpose of realizing their nature, a practice that leads to shape-shifting.

"If you want to know about a frog, mimic the sound made by a frog; become one with that frog's sound. As you tune into it, frequently croak in the way a frog croaks, and all of a sudden it will occur to you what the frog is communicating, and how it uses variances of its same song to communicate different things. You will learn that its *song* is a language. You will discover what its life is like; how it lives in his habitat, and how it functions with others of its kind.

"To learn shapeshifting, then, you fuse yourself to what you want to know. It might be another human being; a particular type of mental state from an animal, a bird, a tree, or whatever you choose. Become one with it. Now you may realize why, on this Path of Soul, your task is to become one with the consciousness of your Wisdom Teacher. Such oneness merges you with the Void.

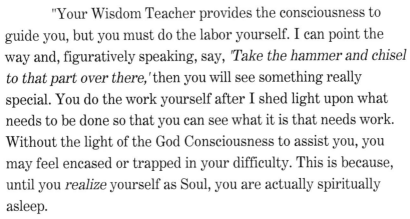

"Your Wisdom Teacher provides the consciousness to guide you, but you must do the labor yourself. I can point the way and, figuratively speaking, say, *'Take the hammer and chisel to that part over there,'* then you will see something really special. You do the work yourself after I shed light upon what needs to be done so that you can see what it is that needs work. Without the light of the God Consciousness to assist you, you may feel encased or trapped in your difficulty. This is because, until you *realize* yourself as Soul, you are actually spiritually asleep.

"There are many people who are asleep out there. People who hurry about to perform their roles in life, and sometimes very successfully, yet live in dysfunctional mental states, carbon copies of their parents and/or other influences that molded them. They behave according to *this* rule or *that* rule, not truly aware of what they are doing, but merely functioning as they have been taught to do.

"As you become your true self, your appearance will change greatly. When you look into the mirror, you may see a different face than the one you wore some years back. Of course, it is the same face, altered by the elimination of limiting mental states. You will see a lightness in your face, freedom.

"To have freedom means that you have willingly accepted responsibility for yourself and for all of your choices. When living freely, you do not pass your responsibilities off onto someone else, because that is a victim's method. Instead, you live a victimless life, because your mental state is aligned to Soul, and nothing else.

"Your mental state is not aligned to a human being. It is aligned to Soul. You begin to realize that this body you have around you, is truly a covering, a vehicle, a sensory machine and you walk around this world using your sensory machine. As Soul, you empower your body to health. You keep it strong naturally. You keep it vibrant in health, naturally. It is your vehicle. It expresses you; you who are Soul. You are not the body. You are Soul using a body and you respectfully care for it. Your body's lips move and its vocal cords move, and words come out, not because you conjure the words ahead of time, because you, as Soul, don't need to conjure words ahead of time. The words you (Soul) want to say, come out naturally.

"The brain is a tool. It is a well-functioning tool for Soul, and you can use it anytime you want. It is alive. It does not have to contract Alzheimer's simply because the disease runs in your family. Its aliveness is not susceptible to disease as most people's are, because it doesn't line up with odd ball mental states. So, it is healthy.

"Your mental states should be free. You must keep your brain and body healthy, by taking vitamins and paying attention to your body's changing signals as you get older, so that if something gets out of order, you can quickly correct the problem. Nurture yourself, not in a sympathetic way where all your attention is on your body. You are Soul. Live as Soul. Your power exists as Soul. There is no greater power than Soul.

"Remember, the feeling body of divine love projects compassion. From this position, there is nothing you cannot do in life, because anything you want to do, you fuse with and it is done. You lock your attention there and it is done. That is why I say to you, anyone can have the Shaman Consciousness or the Christ Consciousness or whatever you choose to call The Consciousness, because we all have the birthright to live as Soul. You simply place your attention at the Third Eye and do not allow it to shift. Fasten it there!

"You have the fate karma to live as Soul. It is the purpose of life. This is most important. The very fact that you are reading this, says that you have the fate karma to live as Soul. If it was not ripe in you, you would not have the book open. It is foolish for you to say, *I'm not worthy of this.'* Of course, you are. You would not be here otherwise. Living empowered as Soul is just *'a couple of inches above your head'.* All you have to do is to wake up and reach to attain it."

Wings of Change: "When one lives as Soul, with Soul directing their brain, does the mind merge with Soul?"

"Before one lives as Soul, the mind is animated by emotional buttons and feelings and habits. You say *'red'*, and a button is pushed and a reaction occurs to the word *'red'.* The reaction would be your preference, and that comes from the experiences you have had in life and other people's attitudes toward that experience, do you see?

"As Soul you can say *'red'* and you have a direct meaning for *'red'* from Soul Itself. It is not dependent upon what happened in the past. It is already freed up from all those mind sets; so, you cannot say that the mind merges with Soul. It expresses Soul, however. It becomes the tool and instrument for which it was originally intended. Soul simply operates it, which means the mind's awareness is unlimited. If you place Soul in charge, your brain is brilliant and powerful, able to grasp difficult concepts on any subject, because Soul Consciousness will naturally enliven a part of the brain that may have never been used.

"The entire brain will be enlivened. This is why, if you went to take an I.Q. test you could jump 40, 50, 60 or more points

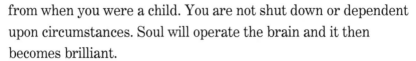
from when you were a child. You are not shut down or dependent upon circumstances. Soul will operate the brain and it then becomes brilliant.

"The mind expresses the imagination in conjunction with the brain. Soul dreams through the imagination or the mind, using the brain. The imagination is the dreaming facility of the brain. I have talked about how this process works in various chapters of this book."

Wings of Change: "What happens when the wires cross, when Soul is operating?"

"The wires are really organic matter. I was using the word wires to illustrate how it works."

Wings of Change: "I know, I just said that...."

"Whatever the situation demands, Soul is alert to take care of it. It is always enlivened, operating in the moment, this moment. And here, I would like to point out that there is no other moment. All moments are now, which is why you may see me jump up from a relaxed pose and attend to something right then, because there is no other moment. The time to deal with something is NOW. When a situation arises, I will almost always deal with it this instant, because this is the moment that will effect the desired result when dealt with.

"The moment you make a decision, you should act upon it in some way. You may not be able to carry it out fully, but you should begin the action. The moment you have a realization of a problem of some kind, that is the moment you should begin to deal with it. Take action; never put it off. Right this instant, when that moment of realization occurs, it should start right then. Pull off the road to the phone booth, or whatever it is you know you need to do.

"This is seeing the big picture and the glitches in the big picture. Somebody might be having a casual conversation with you, and suddenly you see a little glitch in that casual conversation. That little glitch in the picture that is being given that needs to be dealt with right at that time. If it is your responsibility; you have to do it right then. Do not get caught up mentally wrestling with what you know is right, by going back into the mental states that you were given as a child, analyzing this and that. If you know what to do as Soul, do it!

"In the beginning of living as Soul, it is natural to fluctuate. You may go back and forth, back to how you used to see things, versus the way you see them now. You may get confused as to which way to go and, '*Oh, well, how do I handle this?'* But, you'll get the hang of it. One way will work, and the other way will create much chaos. You may make a mistake and choose wrongly; but eventually, you will tire of chaos and follow your intuition. Intuition is Soul's way of nudging you forward. Much of your intuition comes to you through body signals, but that is another subject."

Wings of Change: "Does this mean that one's mind is produced as a result of the brain's responses?"

"We are saying that the mind is stimulated by the imagination. Yes, the imagination is activated by the activity that occurs within the brain. That is why some people have such bizarre fantasies. Sometimes the fantasies are all in one area, because only one area of the brain is being activated. Scientists are only beginning to discover what the brain is about, and the reason for this is, they pursue the knowledge of the brain from a mental state that has a preconceived mindset to it. It has an imagery set to it.

"Einstein often expressed Soul, which is why he was able to understand relativity--your relativity versus my relativity, or the relativity of the brain controlling the mind or the imagination. He understood that. Einstein's discovery was the biggest discovery of the day and scientists are still building their discoveries on those principles.

"When more scientists are able to express their work as Soul, to use the mind and the brain as a tool under Soul's command, then we will know the answer to disease through mental states. People with cancer or multiple sclerosis are mostly experiencing mental states, formed by particular glitches in the brain that produced the imaging state, or the dream state that makes it occur.

"May the blessings be."

"You can never break away from a mental state if you are resisting it. If you are resisting it, you strengthen your bond with it."

Miracles

Winged Wolf: "We are going to talk about a subject that you may only partially grasp in one reading, because your mind will most likely probably get caught up in it, and you will be doing more thinking than listening to my words. But I am going to tell you what I can anyway, with your help. Your help requires that your mind be as still as possible. The only way you will be able to do that, is to find a focal point in the room. I want you to find a spot and not take your eyes off of it until I'm finished speaking.

"I am going to talk to you about miracles and also how miracles relate to companion energy.

"When Jesus stepped upon the water, his disciple Peter was sitting in a boat a short distance away. His hand was reaching out to Jesus, and Jesus walked toward him, the love between them was a force that moved Jesus towards His disciple. The water became solid.

"The world we live in is not solid, nor is it fluid. The earth is whatever your idea of it is, individually and by group agreement. Life only appears a certain way to you because you have been trained to think in that way and to see in that way.... to recognize the world in a certain way. In reality, and there is a reality, a reality that says a limited viewpoint is an illusion; that says life is a dream comprised of individual dreamstuff, and collectively - an individually agreed upon dreamstuff. In reality, the reality of life itself.... the dream itself, as it is perpetuated from the Void or from God, or from Soul, you, has an existence that breathes according to the breath of energy that presented it.

"All things are energy and nothing exists without energy. You may call the energy 'prana,' or by whatever name you like. It does not matter what language you use to describe something, except that language provides a common ground for description, which is important. So, we are going to call miracles, 'miracles,' because ordinary minds see the extraordinary as that.

"A miracle is really a consciousness that has changed to meet the situation, or adapts to meet the situation. Whatever is called for, is done or acquired or enacted upon, because at that particular moment, the attention is fused there. Miracles occur to the ordinary consciousness constantly but the ordinary consciousness can only see the ordinary. When something appears out of the ordinary, it appears weird to the ordinary mind. Nothing is weird, except an aberrated state that produces fear in someone's mind, and then, it is only the aberrated state that is weird congealed by an individual's mind stuff. There are other chapters in this book that shed light on that subject.

"If something appears out of context, we call it a fluke. A miracle is not something taken out of context.

"The fluidity or solidity of the earth is determined by how you approach it. One moment you may approach it one way and it will appear in one way; whereas in another, you may approach it and it will appear differently. You have seen this on special or rare occasions. You will get little glimpses of the shimmering earth and then you rationalize its condition by saying, 'It's the way the sun hit it,' which is true. The shimmering earth may result from the way the sun hit it, but the interaction of those forces at work is a miracle.

"The greatest miracles of all occur between sentient beings. Two or more sentient beings can accomplish tremendous feats, beyond the imaginable, from the ordinary mind point of view, because the ordinary mind only sees things as common or spectacular, sensational or ordinary, whereas the extraordinary

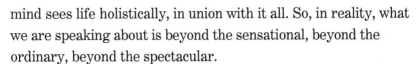

mind sees life holistically, in union with it all. So, in reality, what we are speaking about is beyond the sensational, beyond the ordinary, beyond the spectacular.

"When two or more sentient beings pull a load together, the load is lighter. When two or more sentient beings look in the same direction, what they are looking at becomes greatly magnified, more significant, a greater energy, enlarged and energized by that bonded attention. The object of their attention becomes illuminated by their vision of it, by their vision of looking at something together or listening to something together. We are speaking of companion energy, where the feeling of or towards the object configurates a vision of it. If there is no companion energy between sentient beings, then there will be a fracture or division of what is being seen, rather than an enlargement or magnification.

"To absorb this, please be still.

"A division occurs when one person begins to look at another person, and begins to scrutinize or bring about conflict between them, about what they were looking at, by saying something opposite of what the vision previously was. And when one person is looking at something and the other person sees it in a different way, the energy becomes split. What the other person was looking at then becomes wavy or shaky and the vision that was once held together, begins to crumble apart. So now you know the secret of building something. You also know the secret of destroying something. The karma of constructing or building something in unison with another or others is uplifting; the karma of destruction is depression.

"It is unfortunate that somebody who reads this may share the information out of context with another and then the other may use it for destructive purposes because,

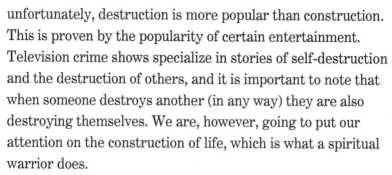

unfortunately, destruction is more popular than construction. This is proven by the popularity of certain entertainment. Television crime shows specialize in stories of self-destruction and the destruction of others, and it is important to note that when someone destroys another (in any way) they are also destroying themselves. We are, however, going to put our attention on the construction of life, which is what a spiritual warrior does.

"Let us get back to the nature of a miracle. When two sentient beings look in the same direction in complete harmony, we call that companion energy and companion energy has a fusion capacity to it that is quite remarkable. Companion energy performs miracles or empowers miracle energy to manifest.

"It may appear that a singular person accomplishes much, but not really. A successful person is one who is surrounded by people willing to be a part of the dream being constructed. A writer has his readers, do you see. When the constructive capacity is enforced through the attention of two or more sentient beings, then limitations are eliminated. In this way, anyone can literally do anything.

"The performance of superhuman feats comes about through the companion energy of those who live as Soul. When a small woman's adrenaline rises to lift a car from her stricken child, you know more than scientific explanations are afoot. Wholeheartedness, single-pointed focus on the moment is what produces such miracles. Once, I saw my little Karin Terrier run straight up a tree after a squirrel, so focused on the squirrel that he did not know he had run up the tree. A moment later he came running down it and then instantly took off into the hills after another squirrel. The question can never be, *Is a feat possible?*, because as soon as the question arises, doubt sets in and it is not possible. Miracles are a product of extraordinary focus, of complete union with the instant being lived. It requires total surrender to the present moment, and it requires a companion energy to fulfill it. My terrier Yoda would not have climbed the tree without the squirrel. A spiritual student learns conscious performance through unification or companion energy with his spiritual teacher. When I entered a cliff at the command to run by my spiritual teacher Alana Spirit Changer, I had no resistance. I was given to the moment, in companion energy with her, therefore, the cliff had no solidness to it. There were no heights to deal with. Up and down were both the same. The height, the ledge and the ground were the same. The distance between them did not exist. The solidness of the rock did not exist.

"I am going to tell you something, and it is very important that you pay close attention: No sentient being can exist by itself, because the dream of life requires companion energy to bind matter. If there were only one sentient being on earth, the earth could not exist. The last sentient being would instantly evaporate and lose its form. There is only form, because a sentient being earned it through karma, through an accumulation of karma and a hardening of his/her karma in mass. It is karma of companion energy that makes situations and feats exist. The situation is the glue to it all.

"To become invisible all a person must do.... all a sentient being must do, is to be so completely still and isolated within themselves, withdrawn from the companion energy of everyone. Then, and only then, can you move freely through a crowd without being seen.

"So you see, there is no big mystery to anything and yet there is, because to live in the way we are discussing, to live in

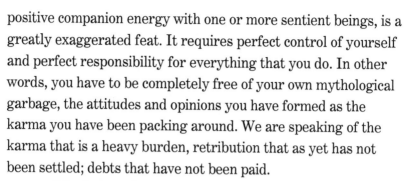

positive companion energy with one or more sentient beings, is a greatly exaggerated feat. It requires perfect control of yourself and perfect responsibility for everything that you do. In other words, you have to be completely free of your own mythological garbage, the attitudes and opinions you have formed as the karma you have been packing around. We are speaking of the karma that is a heavy burden, retribution that as yet has not been settled; debts that have not been paid.

"You have to become completely free of negative karma to work in companion energy, otherwise your companion energy is very limited in what it can accomplish. So you see, one lives in companion energy according to their capacity to do so. This is very important that you grasp such a concept of karmic relativity, and how it either depletes or energizes your capacity to live in companion energy.

"One of the greatest pieces of karmic baggage is the personal ego. *'I want full credit for this.' 'How come I don't get enough recognition for what I do?'* (Pause)

"The greatest companion energy exists in your capacity to project divine love. This is companion energy in its purest form, which means that you then have compassion for all sentient beings. This is the reason you must never deliberately injure another sentient being, whether it be an ant or a mosquito or a dog or a cat or another human being. Always be mindful of this, because even the lower sentient beings can work in companion energy with you. Animals have saved many lives in the wilderness by cuddling up to a human being.

"May the blessings be!"

Freedom From Feelings of Being Trapped

Winged Wolf: "Are you holding onto something you do not want?

"At first glance you may say, *'No'*, but look again. When I was an apprentice under Shaman Alana Spirit Changer, I often complained about circumstances in my life to my teacher - finances, family, relationships, whatever. Without fail, my beloved teacher would look at me in disbelief: *'If you do not want something in your life, why do you hang onto it?'*

"I certainly never looked at myself as one who was hanging onto problems and, at first, I fought her idea that that was what I was doing; but, gradually, as I gave myself over to the Shaman Consciousness, I discovered much about *letting go.*

"One of the first things I discovered was, if I didn't want someone or some situation in my life, to get rid of it, I had to let go of it.

"For instance, letting go or ending a relationship does not mean to smooth things over with a person to make that individual think better of you as you plot to gradually slip away, out of their life. To one on the Path of Soul, this means that, if you don't want someone in your life, you stop responding to that person. Do not write a letter or even send a birthday card to someone you do not want in your life. Also, you should not talk to them unless absolutely necessary, nor should you even allow yourself to think of them. To do so is encouraging them to maintain the connection.

"In a more subtle vein, if you want financial independence, you have to set up the proper conditions in your life. Number one, you must pay your bills and live within your present means until your present means equalizes and, finally, stretches to provide the extended comforts you want. Not paying your bills is negative karma, and claiming bankruptcy does not really free you from that, which is why people who escape paying their bills via bankruptcy often face as much difficulty as those who persevere to pay their debts. Debts are debts, and if you have them, life will extract what you owe in one way or another.

"While you are paying your bills or eliminating your negative financial karma, stretch yourself by studying the qualities of happy, contented affluent people, and by imitating those qualities in your life. But be careful whom you imitate. I can tell you right now that most people who have affluence are not healthy, happy people, because many wealthy people feel they have to manipulate and connive to get what they want. And like any bad debt, manipulating others, and situations, has its price. Those affluent people who are healthy and happy are those who have gained what they wanted by living in service to their fellows, developing their businesses as a service to life, for the good of the whole. In other words, they live in abundance, in all areas of their lives, because it is the natural state of one who walks the Path of Service as Soul.

"*'All of this sounds too simplistic'*, you say. It is simple, although it is not easy. I say to you now that walking the Path of Soul, Living as Soul is the most complex endeavor you will ever encounter.... but, once achieved, provides a magnificent life, a healthy, happy, abundant life.

"What are your feelings of being trapped?

"If you were to chronicle them, you would see by your list that, while the list represents feelings that exist in you, there

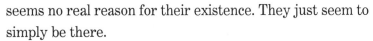

seems no real reason for their existence. They just seem to simply be there.

"There is a reason, however, so please pay attention. All effects, even feelings of effects, have a cause, and **all** causes are scored by mental states.

"Mental states constitute the workings of your brain, which stimulates an electrical charge that produces images on your mental screen or mind, to combine the so-called real and/or imaginary visions of your personal life. They are your way of viewing life. Where do they come from? Now we are getting down to the nature of the substance of your life.

"Before stepping onto the Path of Soul, much of a person's life is reactive, held in captivity by hypnotic stimulus, which is all around us. The hypnotic stimulus I speak of begins in your childhood when you observed and later imitated pronounced parental behavior. If your father reacted strongly to his dinner being late, you, too, are most likely very conscious of what time you eat and feel a bit disturbed about your dinner being served later than usual. If your mother always feared not having enough money, it may also be a fear of yours. Every time such issues come up, you may find that you have an automatic reaction to them. This type of reaction reflects a hypnotized area of your brain that stimulates pictures to appear in your mind to combine a past memory with your present life situation, resulting in a conditioned mental state that dictates your behavior - attitudes and opinions - and shapes your life. To the Shaman Consciousness, you are living your *myth.*

"Life revolves around mental states which propagate one's myth. However, while most people's mental states are hypnotic substances, such conditions can change. Stepping onto the Path of Soul shifts an individual's attention from automatic habitual living to living each moment - moment to moment - from conscious choice. When you do this, you are beginning to live as Soul. Living as Soul naturally frees you from fear and feelings of being trapped.

"May the blessings be."

"Before stepping onto the Path of Soul, much of a person's life is reactive, held in captivity by hypnotic stimulus, which is all around us."

Dream Echoes

Winged Wolf: "Last night we saw a movie, *'A Passage to India,'* and there was something I remembered from seeing it the first time, a long time ago. And I caught it this time as well - dream echoes.

"First, let me tell you that your mind is a dream machine. As your attention is drawn to some person, place or thing, electrical charges ignite the circuitry in your brain -- the right brain to the left brain cross over to make a spark, pictures form out of this electrical charge, from the friction of the movement, and are projected onto the mental screen or what we call the mind.

"Oftentimes, the interactive level of one's brain is controlled by one's desires, opinions and attitudes, which produces fantasy stimuli and aberrated images in the mind. These images project outward to affect the environment and other people (all life forms) within it.

"In *'Passage To India',* when the main character (an English lady) climbed up the mountainside with the East Indian doctor to enter a cave, she flashed on what it would be like to be romantic with the doctor. Her fantasy grew as she entered the cave. As she called out to him, an echo rippled through the cave, not only magnifying her words, but her feelings for the man were projected into the echo. The magnification of her romantic image was so intensified that her illusionary forces resulted in driving her senseless into a dilemma that resulted in resetting the course of her life. The energy of the story made an unusual tale, haunting.

"Life can be likened to a great big echo cave. Anytime an unconscious image comes to mind in a concentrated situation, the forces of illusion are at work to capture the attention. This is why television has become such an excellent sales tool. People give themselves to the illusion on the screen because they feel safe doing so. Advertisers rely on the relaxed consciousness of viewers to infiltrate their messages. Oftentimes they produce scenarios of foodstuffs to implant pleasurable images about their products into the viewer's brain. These images later echo back when the viewer next visits the grocery store.

"All mental images produce an echo in the environment; they actually build the environment itself. This is because the environment is an accumulation of dream images hardened into masses of matter, according to the likeness of a person's mind *stuff*, and this *matter* becomes the setting that the person uses as a place to live. So, when you project images, something occurs in the environment.

"The echo that comes back to you can stir conflicting feelings in your mind. This was what happened to the English lady in the movie. She became so caught up in the confusion of seeing her own reflection that her fantasy stunned her, the impact of which removed her sense of reality.

"People do this in their lives all the time. They continuously produce fantasy images as a form of entertainment, thinking to themselves *'Well, I didn't say it out loud. No one will ever know.'* Yet, something occurs as a result of such fantasies. There is unsettledness, and discontentment. That which is out of balance in an individual clings to the ambiance of their being and it echoes. It reverberates back, a dream echo of sorts, the dream resulting from the succession of images passing through their mind.

"You can see why it is so important to have equanimity within your brain, a calmness where both sides of the brain are in repose. Repose does not mean lack of brilliance, intelligence and creativity, because the calmness I speak of is true brilliance, an increase of brain power.

"When you live in a state of equanimity, something truly wonderful occurs. There is refinement to what you put out. Your mental images become likened to conscious choice and that clarity returns to you in the echo or reverberation of clarity into your life. You are aware of the quality of the echo you project when you act consciously. You can see its immediate effect, and you can see its ripple effect into the environment. The ripple is likened to a cycle, or a continuing echo, a deeper echo, which is the entire field of the present moment, extending a few weeks, a few months, a few years, a lifetime.

"Such cycles of dream echoes are karmic retributions, good or bad, depending on their nature of extension. What you put out returns to you in similar energy. Your mental images flash into the environment. A likeness in energy comes back out from that image; then, a while later, after you think its ripple has dissipated, it comes back again .... and again .... and again into eternity.

"The continuance of the reverberation is related to the clarity of the mental picture that went out, coupled with the intent behind the clarity of the picture and the passion or feeling behind it. So, to say, *'Well, I made amends for so and so,'* you don't know that.

"When you can live in equanimity, you are enlightened. You can see life's clouds as they are forming, and you do have the power to blow the clouds away. You can use images constructively to present your world, rather than have the

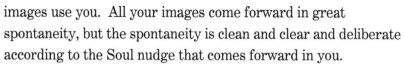

images use you. All your images come forward in great spontaneity, but the spontaneity is clean and clear and deliberate according to the Soul nudge that comes forward in you.

"As Soul, when you spontaneously project an image out into the environment, what comes back is something that is healing and nurturing to your life and to all those who are connected to your life as well - animals, people and insects. All sentient beings then benefit.

"In the movie 'Passage To India', the reverberations of the English woman's feelings were so strong that she believed in the reality of what overcame her, not realizing her feelings produced a *dream* echo. It was not even an original dream, but an echo of the dream. This understanding should make one very cautious of what you put out there so that you can have some say as to how it comes back.

"Sometimes such a dream echo continues for years in a person's life. Somebody says, *'I love this individual. I cannot live without them'*, and they act it out for years and years, feeling dependent, down and miserable, and tormented and, *'Oh, I cannot live without them.'* They are acting out the dream.

"The reverberation of the dream shows one images and he or she responds to those images as they go back and forth, but the dream is not real. It is a dream! An enlightened person recognizes that it is a dream and can select to change, or dissolve it when it gets intense. One can completely dissolve such a dream by removing all feeling from it; it then shuts down.

"Now, we are not talking about a psychological shut-down, which people sometimes do when they have traumas in their lives. Shutting down in that way usually means they are hiding a dream image from themselves, or a part of themselves that was projected out into their environment that they cannot deal with.

"An empowered person does not hide from anything, but rather maintains control of their lives, accepting responsibility for their manifestation of mental images. In other words, Soul is in the seat of power, operating their body as a sensory machine. Soul consciously produces healthy images that benefit all life. As Soul, one lives a life of service - divine love and compassion.

"Life as Soul becomes very, very simple. It is not always easy, but because you are living as Soul, one is careful not to intrude into someone else's mental imagery, which can cause harm or injury. There is an accepted vow by one living as Soul to never intentionally injure another sentient being.

"The sound of the wind is a presentation of the dream. Awareness of the dream is the reverberation from the Void. One can hear that aliveness as he looks out of himself, not *in*. Look out into life.

"People today are usually consumed with looking in at their feelings and many are living unhappily because of it. They live in their emotions (anger, lust, greed, vanity and attachment, and there are some that are very subtle forms of these emotions). Instead, by looking out as Soul, one can see and take charge of what they are doing; therefore, a dream image is not going to escape unnoticed."

Easy Walker: "I understand the echo, the reverberation and the equanimity of one who is trying to live as Soul. When you live as Soul, though I don't see how a reverberation can come back. I just hear the echo."

"The reverberation is a part of that echo."

Easy Walker: " I think I don't know what reverberation means."

"Well, reverberation is..."

Easy Walker: "Because in the movie there was an echo and then there was a long, long, long pause and then all of a sudden..."

"It comes back."

Easy Walker: "...it comes back, so reverberation is coming back."

"When you take an action, there is an immediate reaction (echo) and then, there is silence and then, there is the reverberation and that reverberation is the result of the action. There is always reverberation."

Aims Straight: "When you say, 'emotions,' you're not speaking to feeling, or are you speaking directly to feeling?"

"Emotions are memory feelings or reverberated sensations from the past. They are feelings stored up, that are related to anger, lust, greed and attachment under the guise of personal love. Most people love in a personal way that is filled with attachment; that is, *'I must have.'* or *'I gave to you so that I could feel this.'* Do you see? It's mixed up. It has glue attached to it. *'I love you because....'* That is not really love.

"Divine love is unconditional. It is compassionate and it is joyful. The strings attached to loving someone divinely are joyful strings. They do not control. They do not manipulate. There is acceptance without judgment."

Easy Walker: "It'll be great when we don't have any karma."

"If you had no karma at all, you could not be alive. Soul conscious people project dream images through their aspiration and thereby project their life into the environment, which incurs karma. Do you see? Projecting a dream involves karma, and we have to project dreams in order to live. We live in the dream."

Easy Walker: "There's no karma in living as Soul."

"Yes, there is!"

Easy Walker: "No!

"Yes, there is!" (Laughter)

Easy Walker: "Really?"

"Yes. As I just said, you project a dream image, even if the image is one of divine love, or if you are encouraging someone, or if you go to the store to buy something; that's also a dream image. If you feed an animal; if I go out and feed the horses, I am creating karma.

"There is nothing that you cannot accomplish through your dreams if you are consciously making choices and acting upon them, which animates life. Life is action - a series of images so that you can see events and move around in them. If you were not projecting a dream, you would not be breathing. Your breathing in and breathing out is an action of the primordial dream right there. (Winged Wolf breathes loudly.) That's what keeps this sensory mechanism (the body) alive.

"The air itself is a part of the dream of the Void. Without the dream, which is karma, there is no life. You dreamed your body into the dream. It was your karma, what you accumulated through lifetime after lifetime, that you embody. This is you (pinching the body), your karma, and you need it as a vehicle for Soul to recognize Itself in the experience of life. The reason you have experiences in life is that you are dreaming them as you go.

"Now, when enlightened beings stop dreaming, they collapse the dream. By stopping the dream, they develop no more karma, and so, they are no more as you know them. They become ONE with the VOID. All one needs to do to come back to life again is to begin to dream.

"May the blessings be."

"Life can be likened to a great big echo cave. Anytime an unconscious image comes to mind in a concentrated situation, the forces of illusion are at work to capture the attention."

The Five Powers

Winged Wolf: "Today's talk is called The Five Powers, something that I considered in the middle of the night one night some time ago.

"The first, for lack of a better word, I used the word **faith**. Faith has nothing to do with a belief system. It has to do with an acceptance of the truth within you; something that you know as truth is very firm standing in you. That is faith. Faith is a truth that lives in you, which is expressed through your actions, through your words and in your thoughts. It is a validation that you have that walks with you, and that kind of faith is a very great power indeed. If you did not have that type of faith, you would be perpetually doubting yourself. It is a faith that you must earn, and you earn it through experience.... your experiences. You live, you accumulate experience and you begin to recognize the validation of your experiences, which gives you faith in yourself, faith in your actions and in what you are doing. And that is the first power. Without faith, the other four powers cannot exist, although, really, the powers are interchangeable.

"The second power is **effort**, because it takes effort to have experiences, does it not? In other words, to not hide from new experiences but to accept that you must *experience* in order to find a place for your foot to set down so you can take the next step. It sometimes takes effort in that you would prefer to lie in bed in the morning, or you would prefer having something delicious to eat when you are fasting, you see. It takes effort to decide that you are going to live the teachings. It does not take willpower. Oftentimes people confuse their efforts with their willpower. *'I will succeed, I will succeed,'* and you push and shove and exhaust not only your body but your mind, and some very aggressive cultures today are suffering from pushing in that matter.

"Aggression has nothing to do with effort. Aggression is insisting on something for yourself or for someone else. The only thing that you can insist upon for yourself is impeccability, your own impeccability in whatever it is that you do. But that has nothing to do with pushing or shoving or grabbing or pulling or demanding. So effort must truly be.... if it's effort, it must be an effort of joy. When effort is not a labor of pain, it is not a labor that taxes your body or your mind to its very limit, it becomes a gentle labor of giving into what you want. It is an effortless effort, true effort, of totally letting go, of giving yourself to the direction you are going, giving yourself to the direction you are going. What a great power that is.

"Most people are afraid that, if they do that, they will be controlled by other people, but if you are giving yourself to the direction of where you are going, you can be controlled by no one, because you are in the driver's seat. You make the decision to go forward in your effortless effort. You decide that you are going towards your goal. You decide to surrender to what you want. This means, in that letting go, there is no stress. There is simply a state of being and the state of being becomes a place of spiritual comfort. It becomes both comforting and comfortable, a place of freedom, a place of constant forward movement, one step at a time, sometimes skipping or running and sometimes walking, and sometimes walking very slowly. That part does not matter. Your internal timing of the moment sets the pace of that effortless effort because, remember, the effortless effort has no push, no pull, no shove, no stress. It is a total letting go, therefore if you work with a teacher, you must give yourself to that teacher. You are not giving yourself to a personality; you are giving yourself to the consciousness that you want to wear yourself.

"The third power is **mindfulness**. You must learn to discipline your mind. To discipline your mind means that you decide what pictures are useful to you, and what pictures are destructive to you, on your journey to discover your true identity as Soul. You take a look around you and you decide if a situation uplifts or if it depresses. Above all else, you must use discrimination. Why would you continue to be with people, or stay in situations that continuously make you feel low in self-esteem or belittled around other people. Why would you do that? You should begin to have, in that comfort that you have discovered in your effort, a mindfulness, a watchfulness in your mind, a carefulness that is free from lust or greed or vanity or attachment or anger, because you no longer allow such pictures to live inside of you. Why would you care to allow such pictures to live inside of you? You would not, because of where you are going spiritually. You have made a decision to walk the Path of Soul and to give yourself, to even nurture yourself along that path.

"The mindfulness that you carry about you is an awareness of who you are and where you are going. You are constantly vigilant like a spiritual warrior, constantly on guard, mindful of the input that comes to your mind. You know, you turn on the television set. Is what you are watching something that could be destructive to you, something that would breed fear, breed anger, breed lust, breed vanity, or breed attachment? Some people say they should be able to go anywhere under any influence and not feel any disturbance from it. Well, perhaps idealistically, that is true, when you reach the enlightened state, however, most enlightened people do not hang around such useless forces.

"Most enlightened people live quietly, off in the country to themselves, in a secluded place. They do not seek out entertainment that is filled with lust, anger, greed, vanity or attachment. They do not allow their appetites to control them. To be controlled by an appetite means that you are submerged in one of those mind poisons just mentioned. To allow yourself to feel lustful, and to give in to that lust in any form whatsoever, is to be controlled by what you give in to. The lust that you give into, whether it be sexual desire or food desire or addictive substance of some kind - cigarettes or alcohol, whatever it would be, owns you. You become a slave to it every time you give into it.

"Tantric yoga does not talk about sex as a propagation of enlightenment as many westerners would have you believe. That is a misunderstanding. What it speaks of is a merging of the masculine and feminine energies into the single oneness of the Void. It has nothing to do with the pleasure principles of sex. Do not get confused by hype, books that want to lead you to validate an author's personal play. If you want to know the original teachings and you do not have someone of validity that you can ask, write to me or do some research, but do not take the popular view simply because it is vogue for the time. When you do your research, make sure that, if the text is a translation, that it is written from an enlightened consciousness. Do not ask questions of someone who does not know the answers. Such answers will only feed your own ego and not really benefit you.

"In your mindfulness, be aware of your surroundings. Be always aware of where you place your next step. Is it a step that you really want to take? Is it a step that is taking you closer to your goal or leading you from it? I am not saying that everyone should live in the country right now. At some point you may make that decision for yourself, but the decision will occur naturally. You will know when it is time for you to leave the city. Until then, begin to practice, with great mindfulness, the art of living within the city but not being a part of it.

"The fourth power is the ability to **sit in the silence.** Again, I do not use the word meditation, because it has many stigmas already attached to it and people don't really understand what meditation is. In its truest form, meditation is a living meditation. It is ever conscious; it is a state of awareness, of being spiritually awake in everything you do. You become so awake that, if you are brushing your teeth in that wakefulness, then brushing your teeth is a meditation as well.

"When I speak to you of sitting in the silence, I mean to actually sit still, to be so still that nothing around you is disturbing to you; to give yourself to being still enough that the restlessness that you have carried with you throughout a day, becomes quieted into a state of balance and equanimity so that you can rest. This means that your body can rest, and your mind can rest, and you can live for a while in the *natural state* without illusion being your focus. Life is filled with the illusion that you presented in front of yourself, and also many illusions the person next to you invented, as well as those the person who lives down the street and around the corner invented, do you see?

"Every human being constantly presents illusion, scenarios or objects within the environment as tools for themselves, and they are always trying to sell those tools (products) to the next person, so we have a world full of tools. We begin to think that these tools are real after awhile; that we must have such and such an object in our lives, otherwise our lives could not be normal, or comfortable without it. The more we sit in the silence with our attention focused at the Third Eye, we come to recognize that those things are merely illusions; that we can do well with them or without them. It is all right for us to choose to have possessions in our lives, many possessions for that matter, many objects, but we should not have an attachment to them, because as illusions, they are impermanent. So, therefore, having possessions in this way, we are not tangled up in the mind passions, because we can have without attachment, which is one of the greatest mind passions of them all.

"Without sitting in the silence you can practice all the other three powers but they are powerless. Without sitting in the silence there are no powers. Without being able to dip into that *natural state* of the Void, there is no real joy. Sitting in the silence is what opens the gateway to all powers so do not look at it as something that, *'Oh this is something I have to do and I don't want to.'* Know that you are gaining something very great from it. It is for you, not to prove yourself to your teacher, or to anyone else. And while you are in the silence, look for that place between objects, between patterns, between the light, because all life is light and it is shadow. Between the light, between life, there is a place that we call the natural state and when you learn to tap into It, you will know what power is.

"The fifth power results from sitting in the silence, it results from your faith of knowing where you want to go, from your efforts and your mindfulness. The fifth power is the greatest of them all. It is the power of **wisdom**. Because you have perfected the other four disciplines that give you the power of those disciplines; you now achieve a place of wisdom, to understand which direction to go; to see with great clarity what is occurring in a scene around you; to be able to know how to deal with any situation; to know how everything works; to understand

and grasp the energy of everything that occurs. You can now integrate the teachings into your life and live them consciously, awake in your choices as Soul.... as Soul.... **as Soul.** Therefore the outcome of any situation is always what you know it should be. And there you have the five powers.

"May the blessings be."

"Tantric yoga does not talk about sex as a propagation of enlightenment as many westerners would have you believe. That is a misunderstanding. What it speaks of is a merging of the masculine and feminine energies into the single oneness of the Void."

Knowledge Belts
in the Moment

Winged Wolf: "When I speak to you, I speak to your energy at that moment. So, to recapture a moment from a past moment, is not possible in the ordinary sense. It is only possible to speak to you in this moment with the energy you contain in this moment.

"Often people become confused when they look back into their memory banks, their little history book of experiences, and they recall facts: *'But it was this way or it was that way or I remember that you said this, then...'* Well, *'this, then'* and *'back the way things were'* has nothing to do with the present moment, except as a reference in the evolutionary process. So, we speak to the energy of this moment, always the energy of this moment."

Easy Walker: "To the combined energy of this moment?"

"Do you mean the combination of energy of all of the people who are here?"

Easy Walker: "Yes, and also the combination of past energies."

"That is right. The energy of the past is a part of the present; the present evolves out of the past. You are also correct to imply that the collective energy of those people here is also a part of the energy of this moment. Combined energy, yes, but it is still one energy. We just sang the mantra HŪM together and it was the sound of unified voices. When I look at you, I see you as Soul and everyone else as Soul, as well, so I see the One of all as well as each of you individually. Looking Bear's question about knowledge belts, seems no different to me than your question about oneness. From where I sit, I see it all as the same thing, so both questions can easily be incorporated into this talk. We are talking about energy, the energy of a past moment, which you wanted to recapture, because it transformed you. Your energy had to be lined up in a specific way for me to speak to that energy in you, so that the transformation in you could take place. So I enlivened a knowledge belt in you, so that you could recognize that the interconnectedness of all things is alive right here and now.

"Knowledge belts are nothing more than your own present moment energy, calling out to the historical energy that already exists in this moment. If you reach into a moment with a wondering mind while doing something, all the information that you need to know about what you are doing comes to you. But the knowledge appears only if you are quiet inside, which allows the knowledge to come forth; and if you are willing to be wholehearted in your actions in the moment.

"If, instead of being in tune with what you are doing, you try to do many things at once, then the clarity of actions is liable to become muddled. Sometimes it seems necessary to be doing many things at once, but then don't expect the purity of the moment to come through."

Looking Bear: "You can be generally conscious as well as specifically conscious?"

"Absolutely. The energy of wholeheartedness unfolds itself into all things generally and specifically.... generally in that you would understand the principles of living the knowledge belts, by being able to dip into the historical consciousness that preceded you, that you carry in your energy at that moment. You can tap into the historical energy since it is what your action or your *do* in life propels. As you act, your energy is propelled into motion. And as you proceed to expand yourself, daring to expand, the energy of the historical and future moments jump to the rescue. The knowledge needed becomes available to you because you have aligned yourself to receive it. We are not necessarily referring to what is only already commonly known. You can project ahead to receive knowledge that will be commonly known in the future as a result of pursuits explored today. We are speaking of practical matters, as well as a lofty desire to grasp an understanding about the Void (God). You can gain any knowledge at all. It is all there for you in accordance with your capacity to open yourself to receive it.

"How open can you be? It is your openness, your willingness, that increases this capacity. When you reach out to grasp something, the energy of what you grasp becomes transformed from what it was. This is because the nature of its previous energy evolved into something else, which is the natural movement of ebb and flow or change in life. The energy evolves and in its evolvement, a part of you evolves with it, or your awareness is joined by its movement. This is also how a teacher works. Because a true teacher knows how the universal energy works, she or he can align the student to its mechanism."

Looking Bear: "That's why I need a teacher."

"Yes. The Teacher is necessary. One cannot achieve the process of awakening by oneself, because the individual can only see himself to the degree that he or she is *open*, and *only* to that point. The (spiritual) teacher assists in opening one's karmic doors so that he can receive anything he wants at anytime he wants. This is when one's *little self* can no longer get in the way. That is when a person no longer has boxes in his consciousness to contain him or limit him. When a person is free, he can do anything. Then life becomes fun, or what I would call real fun, joyful.

"The Wisdom Path is serious business, but it is not a heavy business; it is very light. It is very clear, or filled with clarity, and it is very simple. The spiritual life is intricate but not complex, except as the mind tries to make it complex. When you analyze something, you can analyze it into volumes of books. There are billions of books in the world and many reference the same things. You could take any one of these writings and turn it into a book. But what for? It is best that you decipher the writings through your experiences yourself, rather than to rely on another person's point of view.

"Life is fulfilled from your experience with the teachings. Knowledge belts, on any subject whatsoever, are at hand but they must be consciously pursued so that their knowledge can be activated into your activities.

"You have a sensory body and a brain that will do anything, once it gets the little glitches out of the way that say, *'I have to do and think this way, or what I do has to be done a certain way.'* You have to give up rigidity. As long as you have fixed ideas to dictate how your activities have to be carried out, ideas that compartmentalize things, you cannot easily tap into knowledge belts. Maybe you can tap into some of them, sometimes, but only if they fit into the compartments you have already set up.

"There are no dividers, no division, no boxes within the Shaman Consciousness, there is only the whole. So become conscious of what you are doing. Become conscious of the boxes you operate from and then look at the boxes you are conscious of and you decide, *'Well, this way of thinking is not serving me now.'* Or if it does serve you, then use it. *'Well, this would be useful right now, I'm going to use this just to see what happens over here,'* or *'because I know what will happen over here';* then you are conscious. You have to be conscious. And that is what has happened to you (to Easy Walker), you have become conscious of an aspect of yourself and that conscious awareness actually is transforming you."

Easy Walker: "By looking at it, that's amazing."

"By permitting the energy to enliven you as Soul, which is the same thing as *looking at it* but more than that.

"Even Pepy (a burro who lives on Winged Wolf's property) is transformed through the energy of the Void (God) because all life, all things are subject to the same vibrations. And so Pepy's personality has gotten the edges worn off by living here with me. He had been mistreated for fifteen years by a cowboy who did not know he was mistreating him. You know, to the cowboy, Pepy was simply a burro and he used him for cowboy things, roping him from atop a horse. Pepy had become used to having lassoes grabbing at his feet and neck much of the time, dragging him to the ground. So Pepy had many hang-ups when I adopted him. If you went anywhere near his feet, or came at him with a rope in hand, you had to look out. He was conditioned to respond a certain way. He has been with me a few years now and he has become a gentle fellow, a playful imp but a gentle fellow. His behavior changed because here, he is respected as a sentient being; no longer is he tricked or teased or used as an object. He is never abused. This does not mean he could not be ridden; but, if he was to be ridden, he would be ridden in companion energy, without force. (Winged Wolf gazes through the Happy House windows to where Pepy is standing nearby.) Pepy is listening. He has got his big old ears perked, tuned-in to what we are saying. He is a part of this meeting. It is a good thing we have windows on the Happy House, or he would come walking right into the building. (Laughter)

"The instant one begins to abuse people or animals, those people and animals begin to build resentments towards the abuser. The abused develops myths, attitudes and opinions that invent compartments and slots to form a choppy view of the world. So, it is very understandable that people who come here to visit me have many compartments. Many people have been like a *roped burro,* so to speak. You know, they have been abused by others.

"Now, this does not mean that I am going to put you on a cushion and pet you all day. I do not do that with my burro. (Laughter) I might keep you peculiarly active, doing things that will assist you to see yourself, so that you can discover parts of yourself that make you comfortable, confident and strong. *'Hey, this is a peculiar thing that's being done to me, but I am not really being used or abused and it doesn't fit into any of my slots.'*

"The energy that you put out to The Teacher, whatever it would be, is what The Teacher works with. So, I am working from a knowledge belt that I have discovered about you, but it is really a knowledge belt of the Void that tells me about you.

"The energy of the HÜM mantra that we were singing, resounds to different flows, according to the vibration of the Void as it pulses in the moment at hand. The energy that you pulsate into the Void is also a part of the Void (God) energy, even though you may have compartmentalized it. It may not be free, so you cannot have access to the Void. I get in there and I remove the dividers of your compartments. I have a knowledge belt into you because I know you are the Void, just the same as I am. I touch your energy and I know all about you. But I do not change you. I show you what you need to see so that you can decide what you want to keep and what you do not want to keep. If I changed you, it would be like somebody trying to rope a burro. I will confront you with what I see, instead.

"You can use the knowledge belts for anything, anything at all."

Two Eagles: "Was solving the problem of how to change the paper on the bench sander looking into a knowledge belt?" (Referring to some work he had been doing on the Property).

"Absolutely! You put your attention on it and you saw how it operated because you were open to seeing that. Now, people do this unconsciously all the time. The idea is to be conscious. Being conscious puts you into your seat of power."

Easy Walker: "Consciousness is being aware? Is that what you mean by being conscious, aware that you did tap into a knowledge belt?"

"Aware that you are doing it when you do it, not after the fact. It is like consciously going up to a door and turning the knob, opening the door to walk through the doorway, consciously, not merely wandering through a doorway because it is there."

Easy Walker: "I guess being present for me is saying, 'it just happens'."

"No. That is unconsciousness. I want you to be conscious of your actions."

Easy Walker: "But the actual doing of something, like when I had a trailer that I had to connect to the hitch on my van and I couldn't lift it. At one point I focused on the Third Eye, and moments later it happened. I lifted the trailer onto the hitch. To me, it just happened."

"No, that was adrenaline caused by a moment of panic. I want you to be conscious when you spurt adrenaline."

Easy Walker: "That's what you want us to do."

"I want you to be conscious."

Easy Walker: "Okay."

"The Void is conscious. The Void is not unconscious. It just is, but It just **is** consciously. Being conscious is very important, and *consciousness* is what expands the Void, you the Void, me the Void. Consciousness expands. It is the expansion of consciousness that is vital. That is why things never stay the same. There is always an expansion."

Easy Walker: "You talked about the pulse of the Void when we sing HUM (mantra). At that moment is that pulse the same anywhere in the world or is it just here because of our energy?"

"There is always the hundredth monkey principle, meaning that you carry the energy out there, or that it is picked up because of you, do you see? But it begins here, always here, wherever here is since there is really no division of dimensions. In other words, there are many dimensions, but there's only One." *(Winged Wolf laughs)*

Easy Walker: "So if we were at the Isle of Man, for instance, and we were HÜMing, at the same moment we were HÜMing there, the pulse and the variance of the HÜM, would be exactly the same."

"Students of the Path are awakening very rapidly in their spiritual evolvement because of our morning sessions here. When I speak to you, I speak to all of those on the Path of Soul, to anyone who is willing to listen. When I correct you on something and show you something about your myth, I show John Doe, back there in Minnesota, about his, as well. The awakening is spontaneous on many levels in all dimensions because everything is ONE."

Two Eagles: "So there is no there."

Easy Walker: "This is so exciting." (More laughter)

"This is why it is so vital -- so vital -- that we are doing the work we are doing. When you come here, everyone benefits, unless you totally shut down. And even if you totally shut down, you will hear that constant banging at your spiritual door, or the constant spiritual tug, because you are connected by strings of energy to the eternal *everywhere* Void. And no matter how you try to shut down, there IT is. I mean, where can you go? No where!

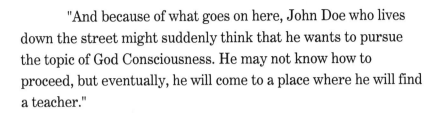

"And because of what goes on here, John Doe who lives down the street might suddenly think that he wants to pursue the topic of God Consciousness. He may not know how to proceed, but eventually, he will come to a place where he will find a teacher."

Easy Walker: "He got the urge."

"He got the urge because of what is going on in the Void here, that he picked up."

Two Eagles: "He has to be open to that urge?"

"He feels the urge, feels the search, the yearning. It is a yearning. There is constant movement.... constant motion.... that naturally comes to you through being open. And you are open because the yearning, while mindful, does not place the mind in charge. The mind becomes quietly observant, yet alive and brilliantly useful.

"The mind is an instrument, a tool for Soul. And that is why I say, do not *stuff* a whole bunch of things into your mind. This does not mean that you should not put useful information into it. But you stop the frenetic stuffing of your mind with this and that, mental gymnastics merely to analyze something for the sake of analyzing it. When your mind gets caught up in analyzation, such as mentalizing, it takes control of the whole operation of your life, and your life then becomes machine like, reactive, and its reactiveness can victimize you.

"Soul perspective can keep the brain functioning in a state of clarity. The brain is only a tool. It does not do well if it is put in charge, to run the show. The mind is like a motion picture screen with replay abilities. The brain summons the mind to image and the image projects outward for us to form what we call an environment to live our lives within the scenes of the images. Naturally, if we are going to live the scenes that our mind projects for us, we want them to be splendid. If accomplished from Soul Consciousness, there is a refinement to the environment of the images we project. Life then becomes what we want it to be.

"Freedom is the name of the game. The ultimate freedom is being consciously in control of your own life, being self-reliant, being so free that nothing can box you in, so that you have access to the Void, and that access is ever-expanding, because there is no end to it.

"Previous spiritual masters are examples for this, because the great masters are continuing to evolve. They did not just end with their lifetime. To study the work of someone who lived two thousand years ago or three thousand years ago, is to see a body of work as far as it could be taken in that lifetime. To see the work that you and I are doing this morning, is to see a body of work that can be taken as far as we can take it at this moment in time. The more open we are, the more we are able to move along in consciousness.

"Buddha Consciousness is still evolving. The Christ Consciousness is still evolving. The Mohammed Consciousness is still evolving, not housed in the same body but it continues through THE consciousness, ITSELF. There is no limit to the expansion of consciousness. To view a teacher as one who has arrived at the ultimate, would be to say that the Void has a stagnant end to IT. And IT does not. The Void is the Godhead of which Buddha is a part, of which Jesus Christ is a part, of which you and I are a part. There is no end to it."

Two Eagles: "If The Void stopped evolving, would life collapse?"

"IT could not stop evolving, so you can't say, 'if'. The dream of life cannot collapse except as you, as a consciousness, collapse your own dream. And as much as you have tried to collapse it, you have not been able to collapse it, because to collapse it, you would have to collapse parts of it that you don't want to let go of.... which may be suicidal. That is what happens. You would lose your capacity to give to love.... to give service.

"I think we have gone as far as we can for now.

"May the blessings be."

"The ultimate freedom is being consciously in control of your own life, being self-reliant, being so free that nothing can box you in, so that you have access to the Void, and that access is ever-expanding, because there is no end to it."

Cycles of Karma

Winged Wolf: "Let's talk about karma and past lives and how those past lives reflect on the present moment.

"You see, most individuals think that a past life means you were somebody totally different from who you are today, and this is not true. While you have been many people, in both genders, and have had roles in previous lives to evolve in consciousness to be where you are today, you *are* still all of those people you were in your past lives. You continue to be connected to your past, and in the same way you are connected to your past, you are connected to your future, by who you aspire to be now.

"When you determine what you want out of life, and you refine and evolve in consciousness, you become *one* with others in consciousness, who have walked and succeeded in their destinies toward the goal you desire. We are speaking of imprints, of which there are many varieties. If you want to be a carpenter and you focus on truly being the best carpenter you can be, you would literally become imprinted by the talents of all of the carpenters who have ever been, and vicariously learn all of their tricks of the trade, as you applied yourself.

"Another example: If you picked up a harmonica, you may feel kind of silly and rinky-dink, as you remember childhood images of the harmonica - wonderful or not wonderful. When you get past your first memories of the harmonica, you may begin to play it again. After awhile, you may notice that, the longer you play the instrument, the more the feeling of the music begins to evolve in you. You begin to play, not so much known popular tunes from a music book, but music that originates from you, a

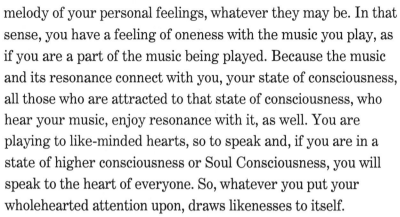

melody of your personal feelings, whatever they may be. In that sense, you have a feeling of oneness with the music you play, as if you are a part of the music being played. Because the music and its resonance connect with you, your state of consciousness, all those who are attracted to that state of consciousness, who hear your music, enjoy resonance with it, as well. You are playing to like-minded hearts, so to speak and, if you are in a state of higher consciousness or Soul Consciousness, you will speak to the heart of everyone. So, whatever you put your wholehearted attention upon, draws likenesses to itself.

"To say that in a past life you were such-and-such a person, is truly unimportant because that person from the past was also a part of the multitude of imprints - past, present and future - that are picked up along the way. All of these imprints give you the identity of who you are becoming. *I am! I am that I am! I am that! I am all things.* I am everyone who sat in the seat where I sit. I am the person where I am walking toward being. I am the consciousness of the Void as It is evolving, as others have been before me. And when I say, 'I', I mean 'you' because you and I are the same. You have a different body, the body of your karma. You live in a different house. You have the house that you live in and the dogs that you have, and the dishes that you have in your cupboard, and they may look a little different from mine, but other than those things, as Soul, we are the same.

"You look as you look, because it is how your karma looks on a body. I look the way I look because it is what my karma looks like. Through all the things that you have done, you look as you look. Through all the things I have done, I look as I look.

"So, in your past life, you may have looked very similar to what you look like now. Maybe in your past life, you did not walk the Path of Soul, but in the days that you have walked the Path of Soul, when you made that determination, you look exactly like that now. Maybe some little things are different about you now, but then, you have accumulated much karma since then.

"We have walked this path many times before together, you and I; not once or twice, but many times. And there have been lifetimes when we did not walk together but we passed each other. We met each other and passed each other because you were doing something else and I was going in another direction. So it has taken us all this time to align our energies to be together again, to finish what we have started. Now mind you, the finish has no end to it. So when I say finish, I only mean to progress, to accomplish from where we left off. There is no end.

"It was not easy to align our energies to return to this place in consciousness to work together again, and that is something to *crow* about. (To an apprentice named Loving Crow, who is seated to Winged Wolf's right). You had to do a great deal of living to return as a student on the Path. You know, at a certain point, when you were a student before, there was a place in the cycle of your life where you could go no further without an interruption. (Pause.) You know that feeling. You have felt it many times in this life, over many things. You progress to a certain point; then, while you want to continue that thing you are doing, you sense you can go no further at that time. So you have to go away and do something else for awhile; and then, gradually, when the energies are right, when you are able to release attachments that bind you, you return to your original intention.

"Alana Spirit Changer, my teacher, made that decision for me on several occasions. She would send me away because I was stuck, or as she put it, I *'couldn't move forward'*. I did not want to be stuck, but I could not unstick myself, so I was sent away to have other life experiences that would unstick me.

Mostly, during those interludes, I felt like I was merely treading water and reflecting, but eventually, I let go of my stuck place, so that I could return to my teacher. I never *lost sight* of my teacher for one instant, even though sometimes I got caught up in anger at being sent away. And that is what you and I have done, through time.

"May the blessings be."

"You look as you look, because it is how your karma looks on a body. I look the way I look because it is what my karma looks like. Through all the things that you have done, you look as you look. Through all the things I have done, I look as I look."

Holes in Space

Winged Wolf: "We previously spoke about seeing life's *big picture* and how the ability to view life's big picture was very closely akin to the viewpoint of the Shaman Consciousness. When I said that, I meant that, when you look at something, you not only see the image of what you are looking at, but also that you perceive the energy of what you are witnessing.

"Energy is perceptible only through openings. For instance, as I look at the blanket that is spread across your lap (looking at an apprentice), there are two focal points; what I refer to as two holes or two openings, both of which equally attract my attention.

"Those two holes or two openings, are openings into fields of energy. Both are folds in your blanket and each has a small dark center leading into it. As I gaze into the dark center of each opening, I perceive an energy of depth, of silence and of infinity.

"The openings in your blanket are similar to openings that can be seen in other people, and in the environment; that is, you see the openings and you can perceive energy through those openings. Openings are neither good nor bad. They simply exist.

"Through an observation of openings as they pertain to an individual's life, one can clearly see what a person is experiencing in his or her life, the nature of one's life experiences, as well as the future experiences one is building by the life being lived in the moment you see him. At a long glance, the entire energy picture of one's life is revealed; or the past, present and future of a community or town, etc.. The big picture is relative because there are openings everywhere.... on a crowded streetcar, a busy airport, the view from high in an airplane gazing upon the world below, or a quiet scene in nature. There are openings everywhere.... in sights, sounds, touch, scents, etc..

"The big picture can be witnessed in openings relative to the Happy House crystal question bowl; those openings on my hand; your head; your little toe; or the opening can relate to the big picture of everything, the whole, the great Void Itself: the *allness* and the *nothing*. Within all, are holes of energy through which we can perceive the nature of what attracts our attention, and this is how the Shaman Consciousness operates within the world.

"By looking deeply into the holes, one who lives in a higher state of consciousness can see the nature of the big picture without getting caught up in the illusion of the picture. What prevents one with higher consciousness from getting caught up in the illusion, is the protection that one has from living with one's attention focused at the Third Eye, where the mind is quiet and unable to conflict. This way, when the attention fastens onto something, an image strikes and the image that strikes, because it is not divided by concept or opinion, reveals the actual energy of the picture viewed.

"May the blessings be."

"Through an observation of openings as they pertain to an individual's life, one can clearly see what a person is experiencing in his or her life."

The Wish-Fulfilling Kingdom
(The Third Eye)

Winged Wolf: "Just as you gave yourself to singing the HÜM this morning and felt the clarity in the air, the brilliance of the light, you gave yourself to the wish-fulfilling kingdom -- the center of your forehead, the throne of Soul, located at the Third Eye.... When you give yourself to that, I mean give yourself to it, then everything you want is given to you. So there has to be no struggle to anything, just give yourself to what you are doing. If there seems to be resistance let go and give yourself to the center of your forehead, to this wish-fulfilling kingdom. (Pause)

"And let it be! This is where everything is taken care of. When your mind struggles to decide what it is that you should say or should not say, then you are not in your wish-fulfilling kingdom.

"You sit on a throne in the center of your forehead, and from that point of view you can say what you want, simply by shifting your attention to whatever it is that you want. Your attention shifts and it **is.** As soon as your attention lights on something, it is becoming manifest. But it can only happen from this wish-fulfilling kingdom, which is located at the Third Eye. If you try to do this by scheming, or setting up conditions of some kind, or manipulating other people, it turns into something that you do not want. From here, at the Third Eye, your wish-fulfilling kingdom, all things are possible -- not some things -- all things.

"But be careful, *look* at only what you want in your life, because whatever draws your attention comes alive in your life. This is why we say, Don't try to visualize what it is that you want. Simply look out of yourself in the moment, and that which holds your attention in the moment is fulfilled. If you try visualization techniques, you are scheming. You are setting up conditions and circumstances and you are not in your kingdom when the plan is laid out. Therefore, what you get, will not be from the power of your kingdom; it will be from your mythical mind, which has dual aspects to it. It will have a good side and it will have a not-so-good side because that's the way the brain works. There will be conflict to it, and the conflict will be fear-based.

"This doesn't mean that, when you're coming from the kingdom of your Third Eye, that sometimes the environment does not present conflict. It may, but you do not have to buy into it. There is the difference. And if you do not buy into it, it cannot really exist for long. This doesn't mean that you will not have things to deal with, but you can always deal with situations from your wish-fulfilling kingdom.

"We are not talking about having three wishes, but any wish; there is no limit, a mere shifting of attention to what you want. So, it is only natural that, if you don't want something, you should not put your attention upon it.

"If you are living from the wish-fulfilling kingdom, you clearly know what you want and what you do not want. And you do not argue within yourself; you simply know what you want and that is where your attention rests. You go about your business, and part of that business is getting ready for what you want. Because you sit on the throne in the wish-fulfilling kingdom, you have the power of attention. You will have whatever it is you want. So, do not worry about how one wish could contradict the other; that is mentalizing things..

"Do not try to visualize results, live in the moment. This moment you can be in your wish-fulfilling kingdom, and for this moment, you should have your attention on what you want. When this moment evolves into becoming another moment, you will have your attention on what it is you want, if you are in your wish-fulfilling kingdom. Then you are always evolving what you want, not something that you do not want. Therefore your life stays on the top of the wave.

"Your life does not have to have highs and lows. It does not have to have sadness, however, it will. But the sadness will come by carrying the burden for other people's sadness, because when you live in the wish-fulfilling kingdom, when you sit on the throne, you live a life of service. A life of service means that you are always one with what you are looking at. Wherever your attention is, you are one with that.

"If you are close to someone who feels great sadness, it is only natural that you will carry a part of that sadness -- not into projection of your life, but as an act of divine love, by assisting them in that moment. But because you sit on the throne, when you leave the person or situation, you do not carry the sadness with you. And when you do not carry their sadness with you, the person also does not carry it as much. They are transformed by your ability to live the moment. It's quite magical to sit on this throne.

"When you try to give service in any other way, it comes from one's little self. It is, *'Oh, I did this or I did not do that.'* There cannot be ego involved; except the grand ego of being one with God -- of which Soul naturally is.

"So sit on the wish-fulfilling throne. Know that it is your throne. You are centered at the Third Eye on your throne as Soul, and as you sit on that throne, you and I are *one*. I sit on

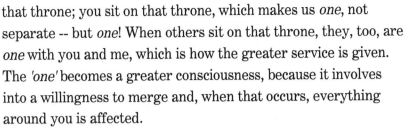

that throne; you sit on that throne, which makes us *one*, not separate -- but *one!* When others sit on that throne, they, too, are *one* with you and me, which is how the greater service is given. The *'one'* becomes a greater consciousness, because it involves into a willingness to merge and, when that occurs, everything around you is affected.

"When you go into town to mail a letter, those who come near you are affected. They are enlivened as Soul, themselves. They are a little lighter because you are sitting on the throne. When you are there, they are on the throne themselves, for just a moment. So find the place inside of you that is very quiet.

"This means life is fun; it is fun; but without mind chatter, without mental comment or binding attitudes about things. Your mind will be miraculously quiet, yet ever-waiting to jump into action. You are on the edge, your energy is contained. Your energy is encapsulated, ready to be activated at any moment. You are on the throne. It is your kingdom.

"Be selective about where you place your attention, otherwise you will lose that kingdom. If you place your attention on something, beneath one who is sitting on the throne at the Third Eye -- by focusing on crime or lust, or something of a lower nature -- you dethrone yourself; you cannot reign from the Third Eye. So keep your attention where it serves you, where it serves the kingdom. Any questions?"

Easy Walker: "Well, I just wonder why I have confused <u>wanting</u> with <u>visualization</u>, because visualization is such a weak presentation of what you want."

"We were taught to visualize. As children we were taught to visualize, to fantasize. Our parents fantasized, even though maybe they said to you, *'Oh, that's a fantasy, that's not real.'* They made real, things that were not real. Their worry and concern over money, were mostly unreal, so they, too, had fantasies, only different ones. And you escaped from their fantasy into another fantasy, a situation that you felt you had to experience, do you see?"

Red Tail Circling: "There were things that were important to me as a child that I wanted, such as a horse, but my father always accused me of being a dreamer. That wasn't so bad, on my part to have that dream."

"Well, he was a dreamer, too. Only his dream said that you cannot have horses... See, his was, *'You cannot do this, you cannot do that.'* You could not accept his fantasy, so you slipped away to make an opposite fantasy, and that was a fantasy from your heart, which you brought to life from your wish-fulfilling kingdom. Having the horse was where your attention rested, and it became a reality. He took his fantasy and he made his real too, which resulted in conflict."

Red Tail Circling: "Yes, there was conflict with him."

"Constant conflict. If he could see you now; everything you have accomplished these past weeks and months and years, would have been impossible from his way of thinking."

Winged Wolf begins singing,

"*Zippidy do dah, zippidy ah.* (laughter), *'My oh my, it's a wonderful day.'* This is not positive thinking, you see; it is direct perception. It is direct attention and the perception that comes from that."

Red Tail Circling: "It wasn't so easy."

"And it wasn't so difficult."

Red Tail Circling: "No, but I..."

"The difficult part was staying focused at the Third Eye and doing it."

Red Tail Circling: "As you said, I just kept my eye on the bull's -eye."

"That's right!" It would have been easy to give up, but you're a spiritual warrior and a spiritual warrior stays in the kingdom."

Red Tail Circling: "I have a teacher who helped me."

"I once had a teacher who helped me, too."

Easy Walker: "ummmm...This is a happy talk today."

"Tell me, why is that?"

Easy Walker: "Well, because of visualizations, and by bringing up the past, I see how my parents raised me and how..."

"They did the best they could, you know."

Easy Walker: "Oh, I understand that, but you know, you said, if I come from the Third Eye, I can have anything I want."

"Yes."

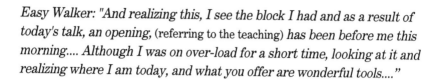

Easy Walker: "And realizing this, I see the block I had and as a result of today's talk, an opening, (referring to the teaching) *has been before me this morning.... Although I was on over-load for a short time, looking at it and realizing where I am today, and what you offer are wonderful tools...."*

"Freedom."

Easy Walker: "Freedom... and I can look at Freedom now.... The question is now answered and I thank you."

"You are welcome.
 "May the blessings be!"

"But be careful, look at only what you want in your life, because whatever draws your attention comes alive in your life."

Ground of Gold

Winged Wolf: "Recently, we spoke about the wish-fulfilling kingdom. We referred to it as the Third Eye. Within the wish-fulfilling kingdom, the ground is gold. The ground of gold provides a very different life than living on ordinary ground.

"To someone who is used to living on ordinary ground, to walk into a land where the ground is gold can be a dazzling experience, because of the beauty of the brilliant ground. When the sun touches the ground, it makes such a startling reflection it hurts your eyes, your whole body tingles with it. It is so exciting; there are many colors bouncing off of it as the rays of sunlight caress it. It can be so startling that one stands there in a daze. *'Oh, this is the golden ground within the wish-fulfilling kingdom. I can't see. It's so bright. What do I do? I better go back and see if I can look in.'* But when the person goes back out and then looks in, it cannot be seen. It is there but it cannot be seen because the person is looking in, rather than looking out. The view is different.

"One can see somebody else walking on the ground of gold, and say, *'Gee, they have it nice. I wish I could have it that nice too,'* or, *'My, they're lucky.'* Sitting on the outside looking in, the people on the inside look ordinary. But when you go back onto the golden ground, which is what happens when you center at the Third Eye, you are dazzled by it. You have to live there awhile to know what it is about.

"It is dazzling. It is beautiful, but after you become accustomed to the dazzle and the beauty of it, you have to learn how to make a life on gold ground. Gold is always shiny. It is always bright. It is always alluring. It is always attractive.

Things that are grown in its soil, are grown differently than in ordinary soil, however, and you have to learn how to do it.... how to cultivate the gold earth.... the ground of gold.... the twenty-four carat ground of gold. It is a stainless gold. It is ultra-pure.

"Gold is different than raw earth. Each has different properties. It has different minerals.... different textures. The nutrients in it are different. When you walk on golden earth, it feels different, because it has a different vibration to it. The vibration is actually a reverberation. It would be like you walked into the center of a ringing crystal bowl. That is what it feels like. The reverberation of beautiful sound is all around you. The reverberation of glorious light is all around you and around everything that you see from where you stand.

"You see the blending of the ONEness of all things. You see the blending of trees and bushes and people and objects of all kinds. Things appear very different when you stand on the ground of gold, so, naturally, life does not work quite the same way as it did on the outside. Out there in the ordinary world, your mind conjures things. You cannot use your mind to conjure anything in the land of gold.

"In the wish-fulfilling land, where the soil is pure gold, all the rules you previously learned are different. Nothing is the same. So you say, '*Well, this worked before, why doesn't it work now?*' It cannot work now. The rules are different. However, what you can have now is something that you could not have before. You can have peace of mind. You can naturally radiate divine love. You can experience real joy. You can have freedom in its ultimate sense, and you can have abundance in all areas of your life; but you cannot, however, have anger and you cannot have greed and you cannot have lust and you cannot have vanity, nor attachment. Anytime you try to claim the land of gold as yours by being attached to it, it disappears and you are back into the ordinary emotional world again.

"When you live within the land of gold, you are a caretaker of it. The longer you are able to live there, the longer you can sustain your life on that ground, which means the more you will learn about it, the more you will learn how to live in such a place. You have spent years living in the ordinary world of mental passions. You know how that works. But the land of gold in this wish-fulfilling place is quite different. So you have to put aside some things that you think you know, in order to learn anew.

"You *think* you know how to make things happen in your life. In the wish-fulfilling land, ground of gold, you live in a place where, wherever your focus goes, you go. You achieve, not through wishing, but through being. Stop wishing..... *Start Being*. Stop trying.... *Start Being*. Anytime you try to manipulate something into happening on the golden soil, you are back into the ordinary world again. There is timing here in the land of gold, an impeccable pristine timing to things, and you wait until you know the time. You feel the movement in your body, in your sensory machine. That is all your body is, a sensory machine. It is like a beacon, only it picks up energy, as well as it projects energy.

"When your body tells you that it is time to act, then act. If you act before that time, then you will have to wait after the action, until the moment is ripe. If you try to push too hard, you may collapse what it is that you are after. You will miss your mark for a time. It is like playing a game and you miss a turn. On the other hand, the rules of life are different on the soil of gold. It is an effortless world. You simply breathe in and you breathe out, and wherever you turn, your attention goes. The sensory machine, your body, brain, mind, projects an image and it becomes solid.

"Timing.... wait for your body to tell you when it is time to look. Now, here is a little catchy part. If you are accustomed to living in the ordinary world and you, by chance, step onto the land of golden soil, you may not be really living from the perspective of Soul, you just stumbled onto the place for a brief time, like *'The Lost Horizon'*, like Shangri-La. The golden soil only exists from the Third Eye viewpoint, where Soul takes command. It cannot stay there if you are operating from your emotions. You will be there and it will suddenly disappear.

"Be quiet. Be empty. As you walk out the door to enter the sunlight to feed the horses in the morning, notice how beautiful it is. Attend to what needs to be done at that time, but be alert to what attracts your attention, as well. Your body will tell you the way to go. You do not have to conjure anything. You can look around and see things that need to be done, and you will do them, see? It will be done because you see it. You are on the soil of gold and you see what is there, what you want to happen will happen; however, if you try to make it happen, to push it, you will return to the ordinary world of mind games again.

"On the Golden Earth, things materialize very quickly. They happen spontaneously, as you set your attention. This does not mean that you will not plan ahead.... You plan, and what you set your sights upon quickly comes about, because you have already set it in motion. You set something in motion through your attention, and when the timing is right, it clicks into place. This is spontaneity. This is what spontaneity really is. Now, if the timing is right and things start to click into place and you interrupt it, you may have to wait awhile, even a long time for the timing to be right again.

"Be careful when you interrupt something. When I say to you to interrupt the flow of mental habits, interrupt that flow, because when you interrupt that flow, it breaks the strength of it. When you are on the land of gold, you should never try to break the strength of where you are. You should know if it is the moment to act and then you will act; but first you must break the hold your mental habits have on you in order to do that. Otherwise, you may think that you are acting out of Soul Consciousness and you are not. You are acting from a reactive mind. Little buttons get pushed, which make a reaction.

"Take command of yourself. You, as Soul, take command of yourself. Do not expect me to do it for you. And when you get into that place, do everything you can to keep away the interruption of your mental reactiveness. You have to catch your buttons, as they are being pushed, many times. Then one day, the cycle stops; it simply isn't there. And when this occurs, then you can sustain your life on the land of gold.

"It is through sustained living.... *sustained living* on the land of gold that you will get to know what living as Soul is all about. Otherwise, you are just a visitor to the golden land of Soul. You are a visitor coming in and being dazzled, by glimmers of Soul Consciousness here and there. *'Oh, this is beautiful. Oh, I had this wonderful experience. Oh, you won't believe what happened to me.'* Well, you will get beyond that, do you see? You get accustomed to living there, so what is happening is not always a surprise. It is glorious all the time.

"It is naturally.... *naturally*.... *naturally* beautiful. You become authentic, *real*.... *real* on that golden ground, not a visitor, not somebody who pops in and pops out. It becomes your home. To make the golden ground your home, learn all you can about it. The learning is infinite. You may never learn it all. It goes on and on and on.... new discoveries constantly.... whereas from the mental point of view, one comes to a point where there are no new discoveries. How many old people have you met who have said *'I already know it all. I'm ready to die. I already know it all.'*

"I live on the land of gold, and I tell you I will never know it all, because as I walk out onto that golden land, it stretches out before me infinitely. It is especially exciting because the land gets to be a deeper, richer, thicker looking gold..... deeper, richer.... always deeper.... always richer, brilliant in a different kind of way.... not new brilliant, not the brilliance of seeing it for the first time, where you have a mental flash as you are looking in. No, when you are there, you live there, and the mind is illuminated and purified just by your existence on the land of gold.

"You can then use your brain in a way that you never could use it before, because the brain is not so busy engaging in senseless things. You can then use your whole brain, not a little portion of the brain, not the average normal 3%, but 99.9%.

"I cannot tell you how far you can go with it, because I'll never find out. As I expand to learn about the land of gold, the Void (God) expands. I am the Void, therefore I am expanding. You are the Void when you come into the realization of it.... which means, when you are willing to live on the land of gold.... *when you are willing.... when you are willing,* when you are not afraid.

"Set boundaries for those people with ordinary consciousness, so they do not take your land or intrude on your privacy; but at the same time, should those people step onto the land of gold, know that on the land of gold, the boundaries are gone, because a natural state exists on the land of gold.

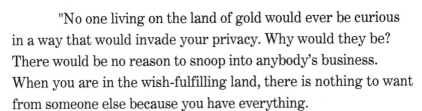
"No one living on the land of gold would ever be curious in a way that would invade your privacy. Why would they be? There would be no reason to snoop into anybody's business. When you are in the wish-fulfilling land, there is nothing to want from someone else because you have everything.

"The only reason one person invades another person's privacy is because one wants what the other person has. One wants to know what is there. It is the only reason one person steals from another person. One wants something they do not have.... Usually, however, one steals from someone who has nothing for them to take.... *like attracts like...* a TV set, a VCR, a camera, big deal. Those things do not mean very much. Yet, while searching for personal meaning, the person may continue to keep looking for something, they keep stealing until, one day, they find out that, what they think is an important possession doesn't mean anything, so the person stops stealing.

"Every time you are able to take a step further, I, too, take a step further. Your gifts are my gifts, because we are all the same. We are not any different, except to the degree of our knowing, our awakefulness. You may be awake on one level, but a part of your sensory machine may not be really awake on yet another. The ground is golden. You have to learn about it.

"You have to get here and live here consistently. Sustain your life on the golden ground, which is the real beginning, living as Soul. Everything else is getting ready to begin.

"This is a very simple path.... not a very easy path, but very simple, intricate but not complex.

"May the blessings be."

Always Becoming

Winged Wolf: "Every time you do something, you grow in what you do, so you know that the sound or vibration of the HÜM, when you sing it, is going to evolve in you, as well. In other words, you can't put something into a box and say, *'This is how something is done'*, because whatever you do reflects you and you are <u>always</u> becoming. On the Path of Soul, you are always becoming. Even though I wear the crown of the Shaman Consciousness, I am always becoming. You are always becoming. There is no arrival point where you put your feet and say, *'Well, I've done it!'*, which should certainly put you at ease to know you do not have to arrive anywhere.... you continue to **become**.

"You just keep moving forward. Sometimes the steps you take are big and sometimes the steps are small, but don't worry about it. Simply take the steps that are there, the steps that feel right to you at the time. So there is no point in resisting anything. There is no reason to run in an opposite direction because, whatever you do, whatever steps you take, will evolve you in the direction you are going.

"Each step you take in life has to take you further on, to the next step. But if you set limitations on yourself and say, *'No, it's supposed to be done this way, and that's the way I'm going to do it,'* then you've put yourself into a little box and you won't feel able to move out of it, so you're stuck. *'Oh, it must be done this way and yet I can't seem to make it work right now.'*

"Well, you can't make it work right now because you are confining yourself. Let go! Relax! Take little steps or big steps. With each step, you're going to evolve into being more of what

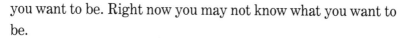

you want to be. Right now you may not know what you want to be.

"It is very simple. You came here terrified, thinking that I was going to growl at you for something you have done. I am not going to growl at you. The only time I growl at people, is if they consistently push against themselves (or someone else). Then, I growl to wake them up, that's all. I don't growl because I am angry. I gave up anger a long time ago. Anger is a *mind passion.* I growl for affect, to wake someone up.

"So, today is just a day of healing for you. As you move your body to do things on the property, move gently. Be comfortable. Nobody is out to get you, least of all, me. This is a gentle Path. It is also a fierce Path sometimes, in its own season.

"The HÜM evolves as it is sung, and you evolve as you walk the Path of Soul. You will find your own excitement on the Path, your own joys, or your own little terrors, and they all are self-created. You are on the Path of love, not emotional love -- not insanity love, not imbalanced love, that can produce anger, only Divine Love. The only thing Divine Love can produce is compassion. And this does not mean that sometimes a loud voice will not come at you, but rather, that the meaning of the loud voice is only to wake you up. It may be me as Soul using a loud voice to wake you up.

"But Soul also uses a quiet voice to wake you up -- mostly that. The world is harsh enough. You have heard so much harshness out there. You don't usually need to hear harshness now.

"You have a spider walking up your arm.... up your neck. (Laughter) You have a buddy. They like the Happy House for some reason. (Winged Wolf points to the ceiling). The spider made a web on the ceiling, then dropped to the floor, wasn't that cute (More laughter). It is making a small web for us -- little strings of companion energy, the spider's web.

"May the blessings be."

"Each step you take in life has to take you further on, to the next step. But if you set limitations on yourself.... then you've put yourself into a little box and you won't feel able to move out of it, so you're stuck."

Grasping the Gold

Winged Wolf: "If you are wholehearted, this moment is the greatest moment of your life. Whole-heartedness propels you into fully living the moment. The energy of wholeheartedness makes it possible for all the nutrients of the earth to rise through the stem of a flower, into the flower itself, to push open a bloom.

"If there was merely half-heartedness in nature's energy, then only some of the nutrients would be drawn from the earth through the stalk, and the plant would not be healthy, do you see? It would not have enough *alive* energy coming into it; it would not fully mature, because maturity comes from the nutrients. A plant is fulfilled when it is ripe of nutrients from the earth.

"In analogy, you as Soul, have all those nutrients rising up in you through your wholeheartedness, and you burst into bloom in this way. This is a Path where you must burst into bloom. The bloom is your empowerment.

"There are some people who step onto the Path and resist the blooming process; they resist wholeheartedness, which brings about the bloom in their lives. Their rational mind reminds them, that anytime they totally gave of themselves, they were abused by other people and situations. The reason the abuse took place, however, was because of their individual karma; it was because the soil in which they were trying to grow, contained toxins of their attitudes and opinions; deeds that were unclean and unclear, which were harmful to themselves and others. Perhaps those people, who are returning into one's life, are propelled to return, by an imprint of the damage you once did to them in this lifetime, even if you were not conscious of it, or even if it occurred in another lifetime.

"So, one's karma has to be first cleared away; the soil has to be renewed. The soil has to be healthy; it is very difficult to draw nutrients from a hard clay soil. It is very difficult to draw nutrients from a soil that is full of strong fertilizer. If the soil was fertilized with horse manure, many flowers would not be able to sustain health due to the richness of it. So, you see, too *rich* a soil can be just as bad as soil that is poor. There has to be a proper balance.

"When the soil is clean, clear, and neutralized, it is very fertile, not imbalanced by too many nutrients of the same kind. Such freedom from imbalance is a time when heavy karmic debts are paid off. It is a time when, if you had injured someone in a past life or in this life, you have paid for that debt; if you have stolen something, it is a time when you have repaid that debt; if you have cheated someone, it is a time when you have repaid that debt -- all your major debts are paid. If you deliberately caused havoc in someone's life to get something for yourself, such selfish energy can sometimes be like an injury to another, and these major debts must be accounted for before the soil can be clean and neutralized, and fertile in a way that it can strengthen the flower, strengthen the plant. The roots can dig into the soil easily, because the soil is aerated; the roots can dig down and draw nutrients from the earth to build a strong stalk with beautiful leaves, and then a flower presents itself.

"Being wholehearted means you are willing to clean the slate of your karma, and sometimes you cannot be wholehearted in what you are doing now, because the slate of your karma is still holding you back.

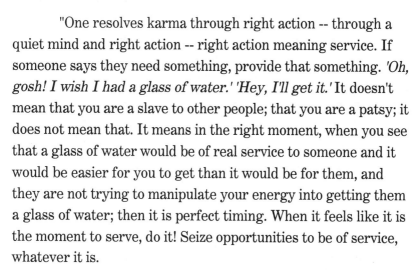

"One resolves karma through right action -- through a quiet mind and right action -- right action meaning service. If someone says they need something, provide that something. *'Oh, gosh! I wish I had a glass of water.' 'Hey, I'll get it.'* It doesn't mean that you are a slave to other people; that you are a patsy; it does not mean that. It means in the right moment, when you see that a glass of water would be of real service to someone and it would be easier for you to get than it would be for them, and they are not trying to manipulate your energy into getting them a glass of water; then it is perfect timing. When it feels like it is the moment to serve, do it! Seize opportunities to be of service, whatever it is.

"If someone on the street asks you for money, do not scrutinize them. If someone asks for something openly, and there is usually a great need; give it to them. Give them what you can from your pocket, without thinking yourself wonderful for doing it.

"Give. Do not weigh the right or wrong of your gift or mull over what you suppose that individual is going to do with the money, even if you feel the person is somebody who has a real 'thirst' for wine. That is their business. Their needy *feeling* is very great. Respond to what is asked in the moment.... *that* is what service is.

"Then, again, you may be thinking the beggar wants a glass of wine, when in truth the beggar wants a sandwich or maybe they have a friend who needs something and the money will help to provide it. It is not your place to judge someone when asked for something. A request for help arises out of neediness, whatever that neediness is, which means - it is a time to give. When you give, you are paying off a karmic debt - something you did incorrectly in the past. The tricky part is *never to give to pay off your debt.... that is not real service.... simply give.*

"Give from your heart, because that is what that moment asks for - that is the only way to pay off your karmic debt. Give wholeheartedly in the moment. Now, maybe, the first time you give, you will remember this talk and you'll say, *'Oh, I don't know if I'm giving from the heart or if I'm giving to pay off a karmic debt.'....* **Just do it!** Do not care which one you are doing. If you do not care which one you are doing, you are giving from the heart.

"Help establish the soil that will grow plants that will have the most beautiful blooms. Let life be what you want it to be. Wholeheartedness means that you are living wholeheartedly in everything you do.

"There is always room for wholeheartedness and wholehearted people. There is no shortage of space for those who are wholehearted. If this room were jam-packed with wholehearted people, we would not be crowded. If this room were jam-packed with half-hearted people, we would be miserable. Can you see why?

"The strength of *wholeheartedness* is enough to purify and soothe the world. One hundred wholehearted people can change the course of our planet, not by doing anything professionally extraordinary, but just by being themselves, being their wholehearted selves. (Long pause)

"Any time you catch yourself *not* being wholehearted, it is *not* a time for you to beat yourself up, because the very fact that you desire to <u>be</u> wholehearted means you are on your way to being it. The person who laughs at wholeheartedness, who *thinks* it is smart to present the illusion of being wholehearted without being so, is a sad person.

"How lost and lonely can anyone be, to think that he can pretend that no one sees his pretense. He can put on a face that is not real and think that no one sees, but a wholehearted person always sees. Their clarity is very great. A wholehearted person can perceive energy by looking at something and by recognizing the nature of it, without one word coming to their mind to describe it. This is called *direct perception*, and results from *Living* as Soul. A wholehearted person is automatically in that seat of power.

"So, when you consider the meaning of whole-heartedness, do not be hard on yourself. You only make it seem more difficult. Instead, be as genuine as you can in the moment.... be as genuine and authentic as you can in the moment.... as natural as you can.... *natural!* Naturalness and wholeheartedness walk hand-in-hand.

"If you want something, reach for it. If you don't, you may be half-hearted or living without heart, without belief in yourself. Do you see? Life is so clear. Life is so simple, intricate but not complicated.

"If you want something and you only think about it, you are not reaching for it. You see, if you want something and are thinking about it.... weighing its worth, and the effort required, you are not reaching for it. You are not being wholehearted. If you want something, put out your hand and reach, stretch yourself to get it. If you cannot quite reach it, that is okay, take a step forward. With the next out-reach, you will grab it. And if you don't, you will in the next step after that.... you will get it. Sooner or later the prize is yours. The gold ring is on your finger. You cannot miss! If you are wholehearted, you cannot lose! The flower that pushes forth from the earth will be magnificent. I promise you!

"I can live to achieve my destiny or I could die for my destiny and the living and the dying are the same, because the wholeheartedness makes the living and the dying ONE. (Long pause). This means in the moment of wholeheartedness, of life and death being ONE, there is no separation of anything; so therefore, there can be no fear. There is no grasping. There is no fear of taking, or receiving. There is only **oneness** with everything, and in that moment of ONENESS, you can look at each other and see that you are all the same, not separate. You have established separate dream worlds to act out your experiences; to prepare the soil for the plants you want to raise. They may be plants that are different from others, but the flowers are no less beautiful. Give yourself to what you want.

"If you want to discuss this, I would be happy to do that with you. If questions are inside of you, ask them so they are no longer inside of you, do you see?"

Wolfsong: "I have a question. I was looking out this morning, when I was out on the grounds; I looked at the pond and I looked at the trees. I want to know, whose mind has manifested this? Let's say this property called Between the Wind.... whose mind has presented this?"

"The Shaman mind has presented this."

Wolfsong: "Your Shaman mind?"

"<u>The</u> Shaman mind."

Wolfsong: "What do you mean by '<u>The</u> Shaman mind?'"

"The mind of the Void has presented this."

Wolfsong: "The mind of the Void?"

"A dream image from the Void."

Wolfsong: "Okay. How does that come about?"

"Well, you will have to have that experience yourself. (Pause). Whatever the Shaman Consciousness puts its attention upon, it *becomes*; it manifests. That is why, too, when you talk to me about things that are happening anywhere, I say, do not bring things to me and tell me things unless you want me to act upon them, because as soon as it is brought to my attention, it will be acted upon.

"If you can resolve an issue yourself then you're better off, because you have resolved it yourself. There will be a greater stir if I touch it. Not because I want to stir anything up, because I don't. It is a part of the job that I have accepted.

"So, whatever The Shaman Consciousness puts Its attention upon, evolves. We needed a place to do the work we are now doing, and here it is. It is a dandy, isn't it?" (Referring to the property called 'Between the Wind').

Kookaburra: "When we are born, do we come in with a purpose, obviously for evolvement, but did I come into life to be a certain thing along those lines, or does destiny happen when we get here?"

"You were born with certain inclinations, interests, desires, attitudes and opinions. Residue left even from past lifetimes formed a picture, and it might all boil down to you being a Zoologist, do you see? Of course, your real purpose in being a Zoologist, is to learn to live as Soul. Being a Zoologist may be your tool to live as Soul. It is good for you to be in your proper

field. That is where you will soar, when you are happiest. (Pause).
Now you have to figure out how to get there, and you will. You
already have the education to get your foot in the door. Once you
get going, you will probably add to that education."

*Wolfsong: "While I'm looking out, desiring to be in the present moment,
out here in the yard, first I'm looking at this and I say, I can be at one, or
attuned to the trees here. I can be attuned to the pond and I was
starting to separate it out. You know, I can be in the present moment
with the insects. I can be in the present moment with the sky. You
know, I'm starting to separate it out. Then I began to feel that, if I
opened that up, I could be in the present moment with all of it at one
time, if I did something, open something... I don't know how to put the
words to it."*

"If you let go of segmented ideas, you could embrace the
wholeness of life. Anytime you have to separate life into little
slots, your brain is saying, *'This is this and this is this and this is
this,'* and you are segmenting the ONE into little language slots.
But, if you let go and just be One with what you are doing, then
the whole environment is a part of the One."

Wolfsong: "So being at One is the looking out."

"Looking out is letting go...looking out is letting go...looking out
is letting go... (Winged Wolf chants the phrase. Everyone chimes in and
follows with laughter).

*Loving Crow: "Another question....You wrote that, 'If you're
halfhearted, you're schizophrenic.' What is the difference between being
schizophrenic, which is being half-hearted, and being insane?"*

"Well, when one is half-hearted, they have a certain amount of control of their world. You know, they have this form of manipulation they have invented that works for them, whether it be a belittling technique where every time certain things came up, they belittled that, so they control that part of their lives by belittling it, do you see? Now this can be done through humor; it can be done through sarcasm; it can be done many different ways.

"So a half-hearted person has learned to juggle things around to maintain a certain amount of balance in their life, not real joy or happiness, because even their happiness is only half-hearted, do you see? But one can do this through juggling it around and that is why I call them schizophrenic. You see, she really wants one thing and does another, but she juggles things so that she does not have to make a real commitment to anything, even though she is miserable because she cannot make a commitment. This is a schizophrenic condition.

"An insane person is one who is out of control. They can be half-hearted one moment and wholehearted another moment, and they can run away the next moment; they can run away and they can run toward what they are running away from; and around them is total chaos. They are controlled by their desire for one thing and their lack of desire for another; there is no glue, no cohesion to their existence at all. An insane person is a person who is out of control of their life. They cannot maintain an image in their mind long enough to have enough balance to live unattended."

Kookaburra: "If someone has hallucinations and believes them wholeheartedly, can they make them real?"

"Well now, what are we talking about? Anything at all? There are little blue men sitting in the room with us, that sort of thing?"

Kookaburra: "I'm talking about my sister. She believes that she is __not__ in touch with God."

"To *not* be in touch with God is to *not* feel in touch with yourself. She must feel no real connection to life or to others. It is a state that you should have a great deal of compassion for."

Kookaburra: "She had a little baby girl at the end of last year and that's helping her."

"Because she's learning about unconditional love. A parent, knows all about unconditional love. It doesn't matter what the child does, even after it grows up. It can throw mud at Mama. It can tell her the most terrible things, but she will always love it, even though she doesn't speak nicely to it; she will always love it; she can't help it. Even if she expresses hate toward the child, you see. Hate and love are flip sides; it doesn't mean anything. (Pause) It is a wonderful experience for your sister. She will come in touch with herself through her baby."

Kookaburra: "Ahh, definitely!"

"Someone who imagines themselves in the midst of little blue men, actually lives that reality, so for them, it is true. But, since they are totally out of control of their reality, they cannot live in the world. If you cannot function, if you cannot walk into the grocery store and buy what you need without having problems, then you are insane. If you feel that someone is chasing you down the aisles or throwing things at you from the shelf to make you buy something, you are insane. You are out of control."

Wolfsong: "Is being out of control manipulation?"

"Manipulation is usually the master tool of a half-hearted person to bring a half-hearted existence under their control -- that's a biggie, isn't it?"

Loving Crow: "Does a half-hearted person have to control?"

"A half-hearted person has to *control* to survive. They have to manipulate, because they are half-hearted."

Loving Crow: "Are they aware they are manipulating?"

"No!"

Loving Crow: "I don't know. I think there are people in my life that seem to be aware of their manipulation."

"They may be aware of it, but they are only aware to a point. They don't see the whole picture; otherwise, they would see that everybody else sees it too. They think that nobody can see them. They think they are invisible and empowered by that manipulation, and they are not."

Loving Crow: "A survival technique..."

"It is a survival technique. It is how they maintain their half-hearted world. Now, if someone is engrossed in maintaining a half-hearted world, he or she does not belong as an apprentice.

He could do the work; it does not matter how much I love someone. He cannot be an apprentice if he is not wholehearted."

Kookaburra: "I'd like to help someone, like my sister, to encourage her to be wholehearted, would that..."

"All you can do.... because you would be resented if you tried to do anything is to be as Soul, without judgment of her. You be wholehearted. Let her have someone to look at, to look out of her little world at, and one day she may say to you, *'How do you do it? How come you're so happy?'* And then you can talk to her about wholeheartedness. When you are wholehearted, you are automatically looking out from the Third Eye; you are in Soul Vision.

    "May the blessings be!"

"One resolves karma through right action -- through a quiet mind and right action -- right action meaning service."

Wake Up!

Winged Wolf: "The process of waking up as Soul is different for everyone, but there are some common denominators.

"One common denominator is coming to a point where you just *'let go'*.... you don't care anymore. You care, but you don't care. You care, because you *have* to move forward, because there is not any way to forget the Path, and you do not care about anything else.... You know, it is like, *'Here I go. I have to continue on.'* And you have to continue because you have been there....

and you have been there....

and you have been there...

and you have been there....

and you have been there....

and you have been there....

"So many times, *you have been there.* You pushed yourself up to the limit, and at the last minute, you did not let go. It was too difficult at that last moment.... It is usually not the easy moments before.... not for someone who has gone so far on the Path....

"It is those final moments. You know, it is the moments just before you enter that grand arena...... It is just before..... you say, *'I can't. I won't. This whole thing is not for me'.* And you take off, and then the rest of your life you look back at yourself running away and you feel cut-off from what you want, because you threw it away.

"So, you come back into another life and you do the same thing up to the same point. When you hit that same point, you can feel a wall. It is like you have come up against this huge barrier, and it seems so dense and solid.

"There is always a way to get through or around an obstacle, and it is usually a very simple way. First, you must relax.

"Pay attention to your life. The simple way around an obstacle is to see that what blocks your Path is your greatest fear - that if you give yourself to what you want, you still may not succeed in attaining it. Lifetime after lifetime, you have run from your promised moment for this reason. It is time for you to stop running, to succeed in gaining your enlightenment.

"May the blessings be."

"It is time for you to stop running, to succeed in gaining your enlightenment."

The Life-Force of Recognizing God

Dreamwalker: "You referred to the life-force in certain talks. Will you describe it more fully? With care in feeding one's life-force, how does one know when one's life-force is being affected positively, giving more vitally or even negatively diminishing?"

Winged Wolf: "So you want to know about the life-force, what strengthens it and what diminishes it.

"The more enjoyment that you have in life.... and I am not speaking of pleasure, which relates to greed and lust and things of that sort, where you are over-indulging your senses to receive bodily pleasures. I am talking about enjoyment, where you are a participant in companion energy with another person or persons, or with nature while you are walking down the street with a joyful feeling inside, which is a love for all life....

"Doing anything joyful, any expression of joy or gratitude, immediately strengthens your life-force.... and that is pretty much the rule of thumb. You can feel it, you know. *'I'm so grateful for life today, because today, I'm going to take this day as far as I can and learn everything that I can. I'm going to give myself to being a living expression of Soul. Therefore, today is magical already. Today is the present moment and I will fill this present moment with all of me, not holding a part back and living in the past - or wondering or worrying about something past. I will live this moment fully.'* You see! What happens when you do that, is your life-force is automatically strengthened.

"You develop a resiliency to bounce back, even though there are still things that you need to take care of; even though there may be difficulties that are not quite resolved, because you are allowing yourself to be joyful in this moment, you are allowing yourself to be *useful*. Being useful in this sense. *Useful*: U-S-E-F-U-L means that you have matched your energy with the divine. You have opened up a part of yourself, all of yourself actually, all of yourself that can receive and give to your fullest capability in this moment. So, you do not do something half-way, you give of yourself wholeheartedly to the best of your ability. When you are wholehearted, the resiliency of your spirit is incredible. You can bounce back from pain and suffering that you have incurred in moments past. You know the reasons for things are not important, even though we think they are. Remember, there are only reasons because you dreamed or invented some sort of motion to occur; meaning, all of life is a dream of your mind pictures projected outward; therefore, the *reason* that is projected outward is also the *reason* of your mind pictures. If you do not like something, you simply change the pictures.

"So, the *reasons* do not matter. You do not have to sit around and say, *'Oh, now why did I present this picture for myself to live in?'* Your mental imagery is like a painting, and then you go inside the painting to live. *'Now, why did I make this picture for myself to live in?'* Stop asking those questions, which is mulling things over in your mind. Simply change the picture!

"*Why* you did something was probably because you were involved with mind passions at the time, or you got too mixed up in somebody else's mental garbage and allowed their mind passions to infiltrate yours. (Looking at Dreamwalker)....You know, sometimes in life, you allow yourself to become involved in someone else's mental baggage because you have an agreement with that person, such as a parent to a child. It can be difficult because, when your child is suffering, you suffer. A spiritual teacher often suffers with the people that she or he works with, as well. So, those type of agreements are things that.... okay, they are there, but they should not block the joy that we feel behind that situation. Do you see?

"So, it is the joy behind that situation that you go ahead and live out. But mostly, if you do not like the world you live in, you change the image that you have projected as your world. Then, you can feel, *'Oh, this is new and exciting and fun;'* fun being a joyful type of fun, not something you are indulging in to make yourself numb to the things that you do not like. Do you see? Being numb is what pleasure does.

"The pleasure of having relationships just to have relationships, and I especially mean those of a sexual nature, but others as well, such as acquaintances and friendships with people who are not compatible with your life, but who you use just to fill an empty space. When you have those kinds of relationships with people you do not really want in your life, but you have them because you do not want to be alone; well then, you are being lustful. And in that type of picture you are taking on somebody else's karma as well. Also, you are making your life-force diminish, because there is a heaviness to it that you have added by going against yourself, against what you really want. That heaviness, as you live it out, depletes your energy.

"Many people live in this condition much of their lives. They get caught up in doing things that they do not want to do, because of other's expectations. It is not that they really want those people in their life; it is that they feel that they have to have them in their life, so they are stuck with them. Well, this is not true.

"You have a right to adjust your life to have it the way you want, and you do that by adjusting your mind pictures, and acting in accordance with them. Now, this does not mean that you do not have to take care of the responsibilities that you previously set up for yourself. Because of the responsibilities that you set up for yourself, you have set a karmic burden into motion that has begun a cycle. That cycle has to come to some sort of fruition. It can come to fruition via the development of another mind picture, do you see? But you must expect that, if you did something that has retribution to it, you will most likely carry that retribution into the next mind picture (life scene or situation) that you present for yourself. So, accept the fact that there is a payback. If you did something really unkind to somebody, deliberately or not deliberately, there is still the retribution. In other words, if you kill someone, even if you did not mean to kill, it does not mean that the victim is any less dead.

"So, you will take that retribution with you into the next mind picture or an entire lifetime(s), and you have to expect that it is going to show up again, only this time you may be accused of murder when you did not do it, but the retribution is there. You are going to have to balance it out somehow. However, when the retribution for previous deeds comes up, if you are living in a state of gratitude and joy and graciousness.... gracious feelings inside of yourself.... the retribution will be more easily handled, except in the case of taking a human life or something else that is real serious. Normal day-to-day type retributions will be more easily handled.

"So, you build your life-force through your joy. If you are living without joy in your life, not only are you destined to suffer, but those around you suffer by accepting you into their lives; so, you are making more negative karma for yourself. Do you see?

"People think that they have to endure suffering, when actually, they are holding themselves and others into a suffering pattern by thinking that way.

(Looking at Dreamwalker)

"You may think you are caring for your son by overly protecting him, but if you do not allow him to have the opportunity to experience life for himself, you are going to suffer because he will suffer from his lack of experience. Even though your child has a handicap, it is your responsibility to make him as independent as possible.

"You keep a child dependent upon you by not encouraging him to do things on his own, because of your fear for him. So, you weaken him in that way. Be careful what you weaken. What you weaken in another person, you also weaken in yourself, which then depletes your life-force. As a result, you may live in drudgery because you think you have to keep this cycle going. Unfortunately the cycle can go on much longer than this lifetime.... It can go on lifetime after lifetime after lifetime.

"Be mindful of the images that you project outward, and the energy behind those images. The energy is what puts smiles or frowns on people's faces. The energy is what builds or destroys. Be aware of what you do, of what you think, of what you project. Learn to become consciously aware of everything you put into motion at all times. This is accomplished by living in Soul Vision, which is being focused at the Third Eye. Being focused at the Third Eye means your peripheral senses are ever so sharp. You see around you. You are aware of where your body is and what it is doing. You are aware of the energy that is coming from you.

"Fear energy is contagious. The fear that you allow to live in yourself is projected outward in the mind pictures that you carry to those who you associate with in your life. Those who you are responsible for will pick up on those fear pictures and as those pictures inhabit you, they will inhabit them as well. As they affect the movements of other people, the energy becomes <u>your</u> energy; do you see, your karma. You put it out there and it comes back; you will pay for it.

"If other's suffer after they leave you, you will pay for it. The pain remains. So, it takes a while. When you release something or someone from your care, where you had fear involved, for a while they will suffer and you will suffer. If while that suffering is going on, you seek the joy behind the suffering, and you encourage that person with, *'I know you can do it!',* you encourage them to step forward. You uplift them with encouragement and to have no more fear; then gradually, that fear that was making them suffer and making you suffer, will disappear. Gradually the karma between you will dissolve in that way.

"It takes a bold and an adventuresome spirit to walk this Path, much bolder than you ever imagined yourself able to be, because the Path of Soul demands your awareness. You place yourself on a tightrope and you say, *'I can walk it',* and you will walk it. If instead, you say inside yourself, *'I'm not sure I can',* you may fall. So you have everything to gain through your wholeheartedness. The only thing you can lose is the uncomfortable circumstance that you now have.

"If you are being impeccable unto yourself, if you are being true unto yourself, you will find freedom. You may stumble, but you will not injure yourself; you may have little difficulties along the way, but your spirit will be strengthened by your boldness. By your daringness to move forward, your vital life-force will become strong and you will not be injured by the fall. Whereas, if you stay where you are, never quite having the courage to walk the tightrope, never to venture into the places of life where you want to live, you will slowly diminish yourself into nothing. As the life-force weakens, there is a probability to disease and long-term ill-health. Another lifetime of suffering comes back after this one because the cycle of suffering has been set into motion.

"The choice is yours. The joy you can experience as Soul is a joy filled with freedom. It is magnificent.

"Life is the result of your presentation of it. You have the power as Soul, as a part of God, as the divine force Itself, to make life what you want it to be. And that is your destiny. It is what you are here to do. You are here to strengthen your life-force, to take that strength and build it as strong as you can in this lifetime! Your strength may take you to the point of recognizing the God-force in yourself, to where you literally realize who you are; to allow the consciousness of who you are to come alive in your life so that all people benefit from your existence.

"To be or not to be! To be happy; to be joyful; to present life vitally alive or to live in drudgery because you think you have to. You do not have to. It is your privilege and right as a human being to first recognize and to then *realize* God, then the real adventure begins.

"May the blessings be!"

Glossary

The definitions given in this glossary are particular to their usage in this book and should not be construed as the single or even most common meaning of a specific term.

Alana Spirit Changer: Winged Wolf's Sioux Shaman Teacher.

Abundance: Balance in giving and receiving; service.

Apprentice: One who, by agreement with The Teacher, is pursuing the Path of Soul.

Astral Plane: The plane of duality that exists in karmic memory.

Attention: The focus of one's energy.

Balance: Freedom from attachment to outcomes.

Between the Wind: The name of Winged Wolf's property; a wilderness place where elder apprentices visit to receive the higher teachings.

Bodhisattva: Enlightenment being.

Chakra: Sanskrit, meaning 'wheel' or 'circle'; term for the centers for subtle or refined energy in the human energy body.

Chaos: The result from unfocused action; an out of control vibration.

Chenrezigs: Tibetan form of Avalokiteshvara, the bodhisattva of compassion.

Clarity: The perspective of seeing life with a quiet mind.

Companion Energy: Being so in tune with another that you resonate together; total acceptance of what is, without opinion or judgment.

Compassion: Caring about the welfare of another without the emotion of attachment.

Consciousness: One's level of awareness of life's dream.

Deity: A representation to which one aspires. A non-living icon.

Direct Perception: Knowing without the need to understand; also recognition with realization.

Divine Love: Soul's feeling mechanism; produces joy, compassion and sense of freedom; accepting life as it is without requiring conditions when giving human love.

Dream: All life as we know it.

Ego: A sense of self.

Elder: Apprentice who has passed their first 100 miles in their apprenticeship with Winged Wolf.

Emotion: Mind Passion - Various forms of anger, lust, greed, vanity and attachment..

Emotional Body: Astral. A place where memories from old feelings reside.

Empowerment: The power that develops as one's myth is exposed, leaving the *'natural'* or authentic self.

Energy: Soul, life force, the movement of atoms and molecules.

Fantasy: A myth made up by the mind; imagination, visualization.

Feeling: A sensation in the present moment.

God/Void/Universe: Reality, the original energy from which Soul and all life evolves.

Gyuto Monks: An order of Tibetan monks who believed in HÜMing from the base chakra up as a necessity for maintaining higher consciousness.

Happy House: A learning room where many of the dialogues with Winged Wolf and apprentices occur; a sitting in the silence room.

HÜM: The sound of the Void; the original sound.

Icon: An image, a representation; a simile or symbol.

Impeccability: When intent and action are one, living wholeheartedly 100% in the present moment.

Journey: A lesson to be lived and experienced, assigned to apprentices and Wisdom Travelers by Winged Wolf to further their progress on the Path.

Joy: The *natural* result of living as Soul.

Kali-Yuga: The end of time when the vibration of the universe has increased to the point of destruction.

Kalpa: World cycle or world age.

Karma: A natural result of an action; a reaction to the stillness; the result of the movement of a cycle.

Kundalini: Sanskrit, meaning 'snake'; energy force in every being coiled at the base of the spine.

Little Self: The expression of being that reflects the myth, ego and/or personality.

Manifestation: Something that takes place while living as Soul and maintaining detachment from the results of desires and goal setting.

Manipulation: Intentional interference with the natural flow or what is; any attempt to control an outcome; shrewd or devious management especially to one's own advantage.

Marpa: Milarepa's teacher.

Mental entrapment: A state of being caught up in one's mind chatter.

Milarepa: Great Tibetan Saint and Poet 1040 - 1143 A.D.; Refer to *Shaman of Tibet* by Winged Wolf.

Mind: A dream projector, a fantasy projector, or a vehicle to express Soul; human consciousness that originates in the brain.

Mind chatter: Internal conversations.

Mind Passions: A mentally invented desire or desires; anger, lust greed, attachment, vanity, and related feelings.

Mind Poisons: See 'Mind Passions'.

Miracle: Results from a changed consciousness; nonordinary reality.

Natural State: Living/Being in the present moment/beyond the sense world.

Omnipresent: Shaman/God/Buddha consciousness, the ability to be everywhere simultaneously via strings of energy.

One: The Void, Soul; we are all one as Soul.

Oozing: An overspilling of energy.

Path of Living Wisdom: Path of Living as Soul.

Paradoxical worlds: Worlds of duality.

Parallax: A mystery or riddle to solve that shifts one's perspective on something, presenting new opportunities that were previously unavailable.

Present moment: Now.

Primordial Teachings: The original teachings of the Jeweled Path of Living Wisdom.

Quiet Mind: Listening to the silence in a relaxed state of consciousness uninterrupted by mind chatter; maintaining silence without will power or mind control.

Reactive Mind: Unconsciously responding to a stimuli.

Reality: Soul, the Void, living wholeheartedly in the present moment.

Resonance: Blending to the One with what is, companion energy.

Reverberation: The movement of energy going out from and returning to us.

Sage: An apprentice who has reached a quality or place of refinement, who has been asked by Winged Wolf to guard the Path of Soul, keeping the teachings pure and has accepted that invitation.

Samadhi: A state of consciousness that lies beyond waking, dreaming and deep sleep; non dualistic state of consciousness; silence; the highest state of awareness.

Sensory Machine: Physical body.

Service: Doing for another or the Path without conditions.

Shaman: Person (Consciousness) who is one with the Void; living as Soul.

Shaman Consciousness: Living as one with the Void, living as Soul; omnipresent.

Shaman Mind: Mind of one who is God-Realized.

Shamanism: To live as Soul in harmony with all life, wholeheartedly in the present moment; one who is a servant of the Void.

Shanunpa: The experience of imitation as communication to live in harmony with all life; achieved through the silence of a quiet mind; to fuse with life.

Sitting in the Silence: Sitting quietly to achieve relationship with the natural state.

Soul: The oneness; the expression of the Void that allows manifestation to occur; the Void made manifest.

Soul Vision: When the attention is placed on the Third Eye/Tisra Til and vision is diffused, creating a state of Heightened Awareness. Living as Soul evolves out of the practice of Soul Vision.

Space: The energy around us.

Spirit: The energy of Soul, the Void. (Also the name of Winged Wolf's horse).

Spiritual Warrior: One who walks the Path of Soul in readiness to maintain balance on the fine line between the world of the senses and the natural state.

Stalking: Imitation of movement to become one with that which is being stalked; useful in the practice of Shanunpa.

Third Eye: Also called Tisra Til; the area above the eyes in the center of the forehead; the eye of Soul.

Translate: Separation of Soul from the physical body, commonly referred to as 'death'.

Unconditional love: Compassion, balance and the recognition of oneness with all life; the blissful state that results when one recognizes all life as Soul; total acceptance of what is.

Vision Quest: Purification of the body and mind to be receptive for a shift in viewpoint that will clarify and illuminate.

Void: Reality, the original energy from which Soul and all life evolves.

Wholeheartedness: Giving 100% to the present moment; intent and action are one.

Wisdom: The knowingness which dictates right action.

Index

Dear Reader.....

Many readers request information concerning on-going programs provided by The Jeweled Path of Living Wisdom including request for apprenticeship under the tutelage of Shaman Wisdom Teacher Winged Wolf. In this regard, we have included answers to the most commonly asked questions we receive.

There is an on-going Empowerment Training program, whereby each month members, called Wisdom Travelers, will receive a monthly audio tape by Winged Wolf, (together with a written transcript), a monthly Question and Answer Study Guide, and a Wisdom Quest to expands the teaching in your everyday experiences.

If you want to be an apprentice to Winged Wolf, the first step necessitates you becoming a Wisdom Traveler. As a Wisdom Traveler, you will serve as an acolyte and trainee for a minimum of one year. It is important for you to know that during this preliminary apprenticeship phase, you will be connected to Winged Wolf by strings of energy, and eligible to receive the Golden Heart Initiation, which is a mystical link with the Primordial Teachings and the Teacher.

Upon year's completion, the next step will entail working one-on-one with Winged Wolf. This is done by filling out an application form together with a letter of intent. Upon Winged Wolf's approval, the one-on-one work begins as a non-resident apprentice.

In a nutshell, the Wisdom Traveler program provides a solid foundation that greatly enhances your work with Shaman Wisdom Teacher Winged Wolf, not only during the first year of journeying (in the form of Wisdom Dialogues), but during your one-on-one work with Winged Wolf, as well. It goes without saying, the Wisdom Traveler program is not adjunct to apprenticeship; but rather an indispensable vital ingredient to advancing your movement to attaining the Shaman Consciousness, and continuing as a Wisdom Traveler.

If you have any further questions about The Jeweled Path of Living Wisdom, please write: P.O. Box 250 Deer Harbor, WA 98243 USA

···

Please Enroll Me!
1-800-336-6015

Wisdom Empowerment Training Program
Membership Form ($18.00 per month includes shipping).

Please Check One:

☐ Quarterly: **$52.00**
☐ Semi-Annual: **$99.00** (New members receive Free Video, *The Sound of the Void*).
☐ Annual: **$198.00** (Annual Membership includes free video, *The Sound of the Void*, and free booklet titled, *The Practice of Shamanism* by Winged Wolf).

NAME: _____PHONE: _____

ADDRESS: _____

CITY: _____STATE: _____ZIP: _____

VISA/MCARD #: _____ EXP. DATE _____

SIGNATURE: _____

The Jeweled Path of Living Wisdom™
• P.O. Box 250 • Deer Harbor, Washington 98243 USA • Phone/Fax (360) 376-3700
E-Mail: tspolw@rockisland.com

Make Check Payable to: HIGHER CONSCIOUSNESS PUBLICATIONS

···

Books

Wisdom Teacher Winged Wolf HHC

The Jeweled Path of Living Wisdom

Videos

filmed in the
Happy House at 'Between the Wind'

$15.00 Each

(Plus $4 Shipping and Handling, $1 each additional)

Winged Wolf HHC

Phone: 1-800-336-6015

- ☐ Doorways Between the Worlds
- ☐ Edge of a Dream
- ☐ The Evolution of a Sentient Being
- ☐ Expulsion of Energy
- ☐ Extension of Awareness
- ☐ The Five Eyes
- ☐ The Five Powers
- ☐ The Forces of Natural Energies
- ☐ The Life Force of Recognizing God
- ☐ Living Art
- ☐ The Living Mandala
- ☐ Longevity of the Brain
- ☐ Mind, The Prisoner of Awareness
- ☐ Pardon: Via La Unknown (Seeing in the Dark)
- ☐ The Path of Soul

- ☐ The Phantom Body
- ☐ The Practice of Shamanism
- ☐ Rainbow Makers
- ☐ Relativity of Life and Dreams
- ☐ Resolving Conflict
- ☐ Service: The Natural Desire
- ☐ Something Moves, Something Flows
- ☐ The Sound of Consciousness
- ☐ The Sound of the Void
- ☐ Spiritualized Consciousness
- ☐ The Amplified Mind
- ☐ The Practice of Living Wisdom
- ☐ The Secret of Bliss
- ☐ The Secret of Contentment
- ☐ Unconditional Consciousness
- ☐ Visions of Thunder
- ☐ Your Karmic Protectors

Mail to: The Jeweled Path of Living Wisdom • P.O. Box 250 • Deer Harbor, WA 98243 USA

The Jeweled Path of Living Wisdom

Audio Tapes

Recorded in the
Happy House at *'Between the Wind'*

$10.00 Each

(Plus $4 Shipping and Handling, $1 each additional)

Winged Wolf HHC

Phone: 1-800-336-6015

☐ Opening of the Wisdom Eye

☐ Living as Soul

☐ Healing Mother Earth

☐ Power of Spoken Word
   Consciousness

☐ Not Getting Caught in Other's

☐ The Hat and the Fantasy

☐ Refining the Personality
   Letting Go of Fear

☐ Messages from Soul
   The Old Man

☐ Parallel Worlds Part One
   Creation

☐ Parallel Worlds Part Two
   Memory

☐ Karma / HÜM: Song

☐ Resolving Karma / HÜM: Song

☐ Light & Darkness / HÜM: Song

☐ Beyond Dualities
   Healing Powers of Soul

☐ The Eternal Dreamer
   The Lover and the Beloved

☐ The Stainless Sky
   Responsibility

☐ Making Yourself Heard
   Spontaneity

☐ Voices in the Night
   Working in Companion Energy

☐ Abundance Turned Excess
   The Fall of Superman

☐ Return to Shangri-La
   Adding Butter to the Flame

☐ Land of No Intelligence
   Mountain of Sand

☐ Mind Gremlins
   Fate Karma Revealed

☐ Accepting What You Want
   The Buzzard and the Eagle

☐ Prayer

☐ Mind vs. Consciousness
   The Dried Up Tree

☐ Deities

- [ ] Stillness
      Face of a Flower

- [ ] Cycles of Karma

- [ ] Divination

- [ ] Steps to Your Destiny
      Textures of Karma

- [ ] One's Degree of Viewpoint

- [ ] The Wish-Fulfilling Kingdom
      Wake Up!

- [ ] Grasping the Gold

- [ ] Knowledge Belts in the Moment

- [ ] Dream Echoes

- [ ] Arenas of Clarity

- [ ] Mind Passions
      Always Becoming

- [ ] Visions and the Natural State /
      Experiencing Unwavering
      Centeredness

- [ ] Life-Force of Recognizing God
      Holes in Space

- [ ] Ground of Gold
      Miracles

- [ ] Ocean of Silence / Path of Soul
      Aligns Six Perfections

- [ ] Listening to Space
      Movement

- [ ] Much Ado About Nothing
      Manifestation

Book, Video and Audio Tape Mail Order Form

Phone Order: 800-336-6015

Name: _____ Phone: ( ) _____

Address: _____

City, State, Zip: _____

Visa/Mastercard No.: _____ Exp. _____

Signature: _____

Checks payable to: HIGHER CONSCIOUSNESS PUBLICATIONS

P.O. Box 250 Deer Harbor, WA 98243 USA
E-Mail: tspolw@rockisland.com

An Invitation...
to sponsor the *Jeweled Path* of
Living Wisdom.

By sponsoring the Jeweled Path of Living Wisdom, you will be helping to propagate the teachings of Living as Soul. And in appreciation for your support, you will receive a free copy of Winged Wolf's booklet, *The Practice of Shamanism*, together with a free newsletter and future newsletters published throughout the year.

I enclose:

☐ $35.00

☐ $_____ Other

Please make checks payable to:
Higher Consciousness Publications

Please Print:

Name: _____

Address: _____

City: _____ State: _____ Zip: _____

Country: _____ E-Mail: _____

The Jeweled Path of Living Wisdom™
P.O. Box 250
Deer Harbor, WA 98243 USA

If you wish to receive a copy of the latest catalog/newsletter
and be placed on our mailing list, please send us this card.

Please Print

Name: _____

Address: _____

City & State: _____

Zip: _____ Country: _____

E-Mail: _____

If you wish to receive a copy of the latest catalog/newsletter
and be placed on our mailing list, please send us this card.

Please Print

Name: _____

Address: _____

City & State: _____

Zip: _____ Country: _____

E-Mail: _____

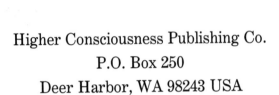

Higher Consciousness Publishing Co.
P.O. Box 250
Deer Harbor, WA 98243 USA

Higher Consciousness Publishing Co.
P.O. Box 250
Deer Harbor, WA 98243 USA